Cuthbertson's Little
Mountain
Bike Book

Cuthbertson's Little
Mountain
Bike Book

Tom Cuthbertson

ILLUSTRATED BY
Rick Morrall

TEN SPEED PRESS

🔟

TEN SPEED PRESS
P.O. Box 7123
Berkeley, CA 94707

FIRST PRINTING, 1992

Some of this material originally appeared in *Anybody's Bike
Book*, revised.

Text and typography by Canterbury Press
Cover design by Nancy Austin
Illustrations by Rick Morrall

Library of Congress Cataloging-in-Publication Data

 Cuthbertson's little mountain bike book / by Tom
Cuthbertson : illustrated by Rick Morrall.
   p. cm.
 ISBN 0-89815-438-3
 1. All terrain bicycles—Maintenance and repair—
Handbooks, manuals, etc. I. Title.
TL430.C88 1991
629.28'722—dc20   91-3884
               CIP

Printed in the United States of America

 2 3 4 5 – 96 95 94

DEDICATION:

For a couple of unsung heroes in the cycling world;
Bob Leibold, of Velo Promo, and Paul Sadoff, the
maker of Rock Lobster frames.

In your own special and different ways, both you guys
have given so much to central California cyclists,
and you seem to get mostly grief in return.
Well, I'm one bike rider who appreciates you.
You make my heart soar like a hawk.

ACKNOWLEDGMENTS:

Thanks to all the folks who helped me put
this book together, including:

Mark and Beri Michel and the Bicycle Trip gang;
Dennis Brady, Matt Kalastro, and the crew at
Another Bike Shop; Adam Henderson of the Bicycle
Center, John Brown of the Family Cycling Center,
Jim Langley of Bicycling Magazine, The Wrecking
Crew and editors at Mountain Bike Action Magazine,
Andrew Muir, Brian Raney, Stacey Campbell,
Jeffrey Hing, Andy Schloss, Paul Sadoff,
Diane Walker, and all the other SCO mountain
bikers who took those Friday rides with us,
and my son, Cory,
who rides too darned fast for me,
but who still shares tips and tricks.

Contents

Introduction

This book is a humble attempt to help you get out of the rat-race of modern civilized life. It's a book about fixing mountain bikes when they break down out in the wilds. I wrote it because I find the paths into the hills around my house a very pleasant alternative to the daily grind. I'd like to help you follow the paths into the open country around where you live. If you follow those paths on a mountain bike, you can get a nice feeling of independence from civilization's woes. This feeling of independence can be greatly enhanced by knowing how to take care of and fix your bike. It's not that hard to work on your bike; YOU CAN DO IT. You don't have to depend on an expert mechanic or guru. Bicycles are simple enough and reliable enough that you can keep your bike going all by yourself, no matter what the rest of the mad-dash world would have you believe.

Needless to say, this little book can't cover every repair for every bike made. But if you use your common sense (one of the few things you have that civilization can't take away from you) you can read the procedures in this book, think a bit, and figure out a solution to your problem that will get you going again, so you can at least ride home. Once there, you can use the help of a full-size bike manual, like *Anybody's Bike Book*, or go to a bike shop for assistance.

Just take this book, a good helmet, and a few tools along on all your rides, and you can head off on any dirt road or trail that's open to you. Do be polite to the other folks out

1

there, though, like hikers and horseback riders. And tread lightly on our mother earth. After all, we don't want to wreak the same kind of havoc being done by the rat-race we're getting away from when we go biking.

1
Getting Set to Ride

To limit your troubles out in the wilds, learn a few Rules of Thumb about your bike and check its condition before you leave on a ride, then ride at sensible times, in sensible areas, and with a sense of your own limitations. That's all simple advice, but the type of advice we tend to forget. So here's a short collection of reminders about your bike and how to use it.

Rules of Thumb

1. In this book, "left side" means the left side of the bike when you are sitting on it facing forward. The same goes for "right side."

2. On most bolts, nuts, and other threaded parts, *clockwise* (which I abbreviate *cl*) tightens, and *counter-clockwise* (*c-cl*) loosens. Note these exceptions: left pedals and some left-side bottom bracket parts. They have left-handed threads, bless their twisted souls; tighten them *c-cl* and loosen them *cl*.

3. All threaded parts are easy to strip. Before putting any two together, make sure they are the same size and thread type; start screwing one into the other BY HAND, slowly. If they resist each other, don't force their relationship. Back off. Get parts that groove before you use tools on them. And use only small tools to tighten up small bolts and nuts. Tightening those 8 and 9 mm nuts takes deftness with the

fingers, not beef with the biceps. Save the beef for the hills.

4. Nine-tenths of the work you do to solve any bike problem goes into finding out just where the problem is. Even if you know what's wrong in a general way, don't start dismantling things until you know exactly what is amiss. You, your bike, and this book must work as a team; look closely at your bike as you go through the Diagnosis or Problems section of the chapter that applies to your problem. Don't work on the bike without looking at the book, and don't read through a whole chapter of the book without looking at your bike. That way no parts will feel left out at the end.

5. Dismantle as little as possible to do any repair. When you have to take something apart, do so slowly, laying the parts out in a neat row, in the order they came off. Work over a rag or a T-shirt or a flat piece of paper or even bark, and put the row of parts on that work surface, so you don't lose parts in the weeds. The more careful you are as you dismantle a unit, the less time it will take to find the parts and put the thing back together.

6. Think twice before attacking rust-frozen parts. Is there any way you can get home without undoing them? If so, try it. You're liable to break those rusty parts as you try to loosen them up, and chances are, you won't have replacements with you.

7. There are lots of ball bearings on a bicycle. Most spend their time racing around in happy circles between *cones* and *cups*. Either the cone or the cup of each bearing unit is usually threaded, so you can adjust how much room the balls have to play in. You don't want too much play; just enough to let the balls roll smoothly. To adjust any bearing

set, first loosen (c-cl, usually) the locknut or lockring that holds the whole unit in place, then tighten (usually cl) the threaded part that's easiest to get at until you feel it squeeze the ball bearings. Then back it off (c-cl) a bit; usually less than a quarter turn is enough. Finally, re-tighten the locknut or ring (cl) so everything stays nicely adjusted. Spin the part on its bearings. It should coast smoothly and gradually to a stop. See if you can wiggle it from side to side on the bearings. If it is free to wiggle more than a hair's breadth, or if it is not free to roll smoothly, readjust the thing. Keep those bearings oiled or greased, adjusted, and out of the rain, and they'll give you years of happy, free-rolling service. If your bike gets covered with mud or gritty dust, you can wash it off, but don't aim powerful blasts of water, especially water with detergent in it (like at a do-it-yourself carwash) at any of the bearings. You can ruin bearings by washing the lubricant out of them; even "sealed" bearings can be ruined in this way.

8. Cultivate a keen ear for those little complaining noises your bike makes when it has problems, like grindy bearings, or a kerchunking chain, or a slight creak-squeaking of a crank that is coming loose. You don't have to talk to your bike when you ride it—just listen to it affectionately, and take care of its minor complaints before they become major problems miles away from home.

9. Find a good bike shop in the area where you do most of your riding. Good shops are not necessarily the big flashy ones; they are the ones with people who *care*. Do as much of your bike shopping as you can at a shop that cares, and send friends to get their bikes there. The prices may be a bit higher, but the value is higher in the long run.

10. If you need help out in the wilds, don't be afraid to ask for it. Use discretion with strangers if you are riding alone, but if you are in a group, don't be shy about asking folks if you can use their tools or make a phone call. You'll be amazed at how many friendly folks there are out there; all you have to do is show a little courtesy.

When and Where to Ride

Ride during the daytime on trails or dirt roads where bikes are allowed. Don't ride on high ridges in lightning storms, don't ride in desert gullies during downpours, keep off farms where the farmers tend to shower visitors with shotgun pellets, and don't ride in blizzards at night, unless you are an insomniac survivalist. Just ride wherever and whenever it makes sense to. The point is to keep damage to yourself and hassles with your bike to a minimum.

Quick Maintenance Check

When you're itching to go on a ride, you don't want to spend much time fooling around with your bike. Just check the following three items and you'll cover about nine-tenths of the causes for trouble encountered on mountain bike rides.

1. Chain: Make sure it is clean and lubricated. Check it for excessive stretching and kinks, too. (See page 103)

2. Tires: Make sure they're pumped up to the correct pressure and make sure the tube isn't bulging out anywhere. (See page 60)

3. Brakes: Make sure they'll stop you. When you squeeze the levers, they should only go about two-thirds of the way to the handlebars before the brakes are fully applied. Check for frayed cables and loose or cockeyed brake shoes (see pages 19 and 26).

Those are the most important items. There are a few other things you can look into if you have been getting any hints of trouble on previous rides. If your gears have been slipping or making weird noises, check the cables and adjustment. (See page 114) If your cranks have been squeaking, check the mounting bolts for looseness (page 93); if your wheels are loose, tighten the nuts or the quick-release lever (page 64), or adjust the bearings (page 65). Check your seat (page 82), handlebars (page 30), and headset (page 36) for looseness, too.

Tools and Other Stuff to Take

You can't take every tool and spare part you might need for every imaginable repair. Take the mini-kit (following) on short rides, and put together a maxi-kit for longer treks or mountain bike tours. No matter what size ride you're going on, wear a helmet. If you protect and use the gray matter inside your helmet, it will help you work out makeshift solutions to your bike problems with the tools you have at hand. That gray stuff can get you out of a lot of jams, even when you don't have the best tools along. And you'll find that gray matter, unlike most tools, improves with use under pressure.

HELMET

GRAY MATTER

MINI-KIT

1. Adjustable Wrench (crescent wrench). Get a good one. Attributes of a good one are a forged body, milled and hardened jaws, and a precise adjusting action. To test a wrench, open the adjustable jaw a little and see if you can wiggle it in such a way that it moves up and down in relation to the body of the tool. A good adjustable wrench will wiggle very little, and the jaws will stay parallel. The six-inch size is best. Some people hacksaw the end of the handle off to make it even smaller.

2. Screwdriver/Pocket Knife. A screwdriver with a forged steel shank and a thin blade end is best. A pocket knife with a screwdriver blade will work fine for most adjusting screws, and it's good to have a knife for things like slicing cheese for lunch out in the wilds. Just don't do any heavy prying or tire-removing (see below) with your pocket knife or screwdriver blade. The screwdriver tip should be ¼ inch wide and the shank 4 or 5 inches long.

3. Tire Patch Kit and Tire Irons. The patch kit can be bought as a unit from any bike shop. It should have a tube of glue (keep the cap on tight or the glue dries up), several small and large patches (the kind that taper out to thin, flexible edges are best), and something to scrape a rough spot on the tube, like a swatch of rough sandpaper. Add a boot to your patch kit; to make one, cut out a ¾ inch by 3 inch piece of thin sidewall from an old tire. You can use it to cover a bad slit in it, or at least make the slit tire usable to get you home. Each tire iron should have a thin, smooth, rounded prying end, and a hook on the other end to fit onto a spoke after you have pried up on your tire bead. Make sure the tire irons are top quality, either steel or heavy-duty plastic; cheapo thick or sharp-edged ones make holes in your tube like a screwdriver if you don't use them just right.

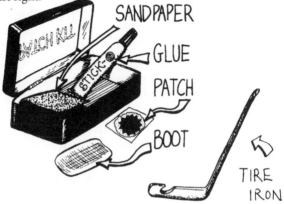

4. *Spare Tube.* It can be a lightweight one; rolled up tightly, it will fit in the small pouch you use to carry your mini-kit.

5. *Allen Keys.* Depending on what kind of equipment you have, you may need sizes ranging from 1.5 mm to 6 mm. Some bikes have parts that require ⅛-inch and other American size keys. If you get a new part that requires an odd-size allen wrench, buy the wrench at the same time you get the part, and add the wrench to your mini-kit. (I keep all mine together with a red rubber band so I don't lose the little buggers.)

6. Chain Tool. For driving rivets in and out of the chain. Get one that is the right size for your width of chain, either standard or narrow. Inexpensive ones work, but don't last long. Save the spare tip if one comes with yours; the tip tends to pop out of the tool and get lost. If you're plagued with tip loss, you can spend a lot of money on a heavy-duty plier-type chain tool, or you can keep a close eye on the tip of your cheap chain tool; when you see it flaring out like the butt end of a wedge where it's been hammered, carefully file that flare off with a small metal file, so the tip won't get stuck inside the chain's sideplates.

7. Tire Pump. Get either a well-made bike frame pump, a strong mini-pump, an inside-the-seat post pump, or a CO$_2$ tire inflater. It can be small, as long as it has a head that fits securely on your tire valves, and solid working parts that won't fail when you really need them. Many mountain bikers carry mini-pumps or CO$_2$ pumps in their fanny packs; they run no risk of the pump getting joggled off their bike frame, and they run no risk of having the pump stolen if they leave the bike unattended. The kind of pump that becomes a part of your seat post is another good solution; if you get one with a little hose, though, make sure you take care of the little hose so it doesn't break or get clogged. If you get

Mini Pump

lots of flats and need a full-size frame pump, strap it to the frame with a velcro-binding pump strap so it can't get joggled off.

8. Friend. No description needed. Take a good one on all long rides for parts-holding, morale-boosting, and, if things get really bad, help-fetching.

9. A quarter and a couple of dollars. Not as important as a friend, especially when you are far from civilization. But handy for calling home from the nearest gas station, or buying emergency food from country stores.

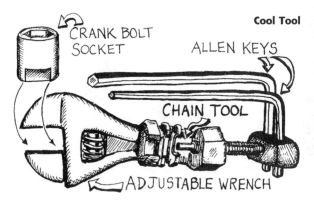

Cool Tool

CRANK BOLT SOCKET

ALLEN KEYS

CHAIN TOOL

ADJUSTABLE WRENCH

You can put all the tools in the mini-kit inside a small cloth pouch, and strap it to the rails under your seat. There are even multi-tools, such as the Cool Tool, that combine things like a wrench, chain-tool, allen keys, headset wrench, and other tools, so you can save weight and bulk in your mini-kit. The Cool Tool works well for many jobs if you use it very carefully, but most other multi-tools are so poorly designed they are not worth including in your kit.

MAXI-KIT (items to include for long treks, rough conditions)

10. Cable Cutters. The best type is the heavy-duty bicycle cable clipper that grabs the cable in a diamond-shaped hole and shears it off clean. Park Tool Co. makes a great cable cutter. Expensive, but worth it. The chomping types of wire cutters (such as those on needlenose pliers and diagonal cutters) will do, but if they are dull or flimsy, they mash the ends of the cables; you have to thread the cables through their housings before you cut them to size, and re-threading is a real pain.

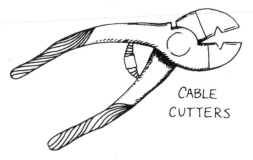

CABLE
CUTTERS

11. Pliers. The hardware-store variety are OK. Channel lock pliers are better. To be used only as directed. NOT a valid replacement for a good crescent wrench.

12. Lubricants. Light oil or bike lubricant such as Triflow or TetraBike for your chain and other moving parts. You can get very small containers of some lubricants, perfect for stuffing in your tool bag, even in a mini-kit.

13. Hub Spanners. Buy a set of two that fit your hubs, either a 13-14 mm set, or a 15-16 mm set. Campagnolo and Park make good ones. They cost a lot, but they are essential to wheel bearing adjustment.

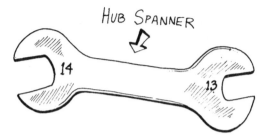

14. *Spoke Wrench*. A cheap little tool that can get you into a lot of expensive trouble. That's why they're so cheap, and available at any bike shop which will take on a wheel you ruin. So use only as directed. The Spokey type works well, as long as it is the right size for your spoke nipples.

15. *"Y" Socket Tool*. A nifty little thing that fits easily in your hand, fits all of the 8, 9, and 10 mm bolts and nuts on bikes, and gives you enough leverage to tighten them, but not strip them, if you take it easy.

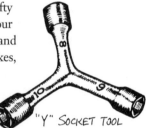

16. *Headset Spanner*. You can get an attachment for a Cool Tool that will work OK if you don't torque on it too hard. A full-size spanner is a big, heavy, one-use tool; the kind I like to avoid taking on rides with me if I can. A good option is to get a good, nonaluminum head-set, adjust it well at home, and take the Cool Tool gizmo for emergencies.

17. *Spare Parts*. Spokes (exactly the same sizes as the ones on your wheels, of course), brake and gear cables, a few links of chain, and maybe an elastic "bungee" cord or two.

FOUND AND BORROWED TOOLS

You'll be amazed at the things you can use for tools if you're stuck out in the middle of nowhere. A rock becomes a hammer or an anvil. A stick becomes a lever. A tree limb becomes a bikestand. And then there are the primitive tools that you can borrow from a friendly farmer or woodsperson. I've met many farmers who chased me off their land for trespassing, but I've never met a country mechanic who wouldn't let me use a monkey wrench or a pair of channel lock pliers. In fact, I have more trouble trying to politely tell mechanics that I would prefer to fix the bike myself, rather than turn it over to them. I'll never forget the guy who wanted to take his welding torch to my bent Cinelli forks.

2
Brakes

OVERALL BRAKE SYSTEM DIAGNOSIS: If you are having problems with your brakes, you may have to look at the whole brake system to find out just what is causing the problem. The following paragraphs describe the two basic problems you can have with brakes, and help you find out which part of the brake system you have to work on.

Brakes don't go on. The problem is probably a loose or broken cable, or an entire brake system that is so rusty or mud-clogged that the parts are locked together. Inspect the brake cable for breaks or frayed places; see Brake Cables PROBLEMS for more info. If the whole system for either your front or your back brake is rusty or clogged, try cleaning it with a rag or your shirt-tail, apply some lubricant if you have any along, and work the mechanism by hand while squeezing the hand lever; if that doesn't get it working, ride home slowly using your other brake, then refer to a shop manual for information on how to do a complete brake overhaul.

Brakes don't go off. Something is stuck somewhere in your brake system so one or both of the brake shoes won't let go of the wheel rim when you let go of the brake handle. Any of the three units of the brake system, the hand lever, the cable, or the mechanism could be hung up. If your brakes get the "stickies" (a malady about as common to brakes as the common cold is to man), first find out which unit is stuck. Apply the brake. Move the hand lever back to its released position. If it moves freely, it's OK and you know the snag is in the cable and/or the mechanism. If the hand lever doesn't move freely, it has the stickies (see Hand Lever PROBLEMS).

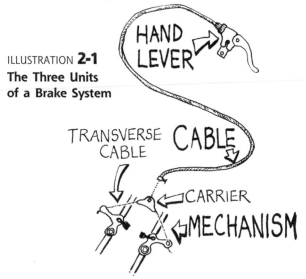

ILLUSTRATION **2-1**
**The Three Units
of a Brake System**

If the trouble is in the cable or mechanism, pull the little transverse cable end out of its notch on one of the cantilevers so the brakes become loose. Then tug a little on the carrier with one hand and operate the brake hand lever with the other hand. When you release the lever, does the cable fail to slip back towards your tugging hand? If so, and the lever is OK, then you can bet the cable has the stickies. See Brake Cables PROBLEMS.

Cable OK? That leaves the brake mechanism. Try reaching through the spokes of the wheel with your fingers and squeezing and releasing the brake cantilevers. If one or both don't spring away from the rim when you let go of them, or if one shoe is cockeyed, see Mechanism PROBLEMS.

If you have problems other than the two above, see the unit that has a problem; for example, if you can't reach the lever because your fingers are too short, see the *Hand Lever* section below.

Hand Lever

PROBLEMS: *Stickies.* If you have taken a spill, the problem is usually a bent lever, or dirt stuck in the part of the lever where it pivots. See if the lever is twisted out of line. Compare it with the other one. Try to straighten it with your bare hands, holding the part that mounts to the handlebar in one hand and bending the lever with the other. Just straighten it enough to get you home. If it seems weak or still partially sticky, make sure you replace the whole unit before your next ride. You don't want that brake to break the next time you really need it.

If the pivot seems clogged with dirt or if it has tightened up, loosen (c-cl) the pivot bolt. Loosen it about two turns. Then work the lever back and forth a bunch of times to work out any dirt in there. If you have some lubricant with you, squirt a dab in there. Then tighten (cl) the bolt. If the lever action gets stiff, back off (c-cl) the pivot bolt a quarter turn or so. Most pivot bolts have self-locking nuts, so they don't come loose if you don't tighten them up all the way. Even if the pivot bolt is loose after you back it off a bit, it will probably stay in there until you get home. Just make

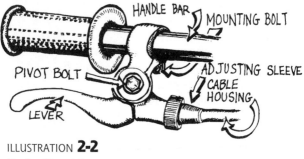

ILLUSTRATION **2-2**
Brake Hand Lever

sure you take the brake lever apart when you get there; clean it and replace any bent or munched parts, then reassemble it.

If the *whole hand lever is loose*, so it slips around on the handlebars, you have to tighten (cl) the mounting bolt that holds it. On most brake hand levers, you need an allen key to do the tightening. If the hand lever slips out of place while it is loose, get it lined up like the other one, then tighten (cl) the mounting bolt firmly.

If you *can't reach the hand lever* because your fingers are too short or the lever sticks out too far, first loosen the brakes a little (see *Adjusting the Brakes* below) then look on or under the main body of the hand lever unit and see if there is a screw or an allen bolt that doesn't have an obvious purpose. Turn the screw or bolt (if your brakes have one), and you should see the hand lever move closer or farther from the handlebars. Fiddle with the screw or bolt until the lever is just close enough for you to reach and no closer. Readjust the brakes if they are too tight now.

Brake Cables

PROBLEMS: *Brakes loose.* You are screaming down Kamikaze at Mammoth and you come flying around a blind curve just a wee bit too fast, and suddenly find that you are heading for a bathtub-sized boulder. You slam on the brakes. Nothing happens for a terribly long instant. The next thing you realize is that the ground is coming up at you. Agh. Avoid this scenario. Keep your brakes adjusted.

Adjusting the brakes means tightening the cable so you only have to squeeze the lever about halfway to the handlebars to apply them fully. Some people (and I'm one of them) like their brakes a bit looser than this, so the lever goes most of the way to the handlebar before the brakes are fully applied. This makes sense, because it lets you grip the bars with most of your fingers while applying the brakes with just two slightly extended fingers. Short, "two-finger" brake hand levers are good for the same reason, as long as they give you enough leverage. But no matter what your brake set-up, you should never let either brake get so loose that the handle goes all the way to the handlebar without stopping the wheel. Loose brakes are especially dangerous on a mountain bike because if the transverse cable gets so loose that it jumps out of the carrier or flops down on the tire, it can catch on the nobbies, which slams on the brake. If this happens on your front wheel, you endo (like, you flip; do a head-plant; auger into the dirt). This is a most unpleasant way to learn that your brakes need adjustment.

A *minor adjustment* will usually be enough to get you home. See if there is an adjusting sleeve on your brake handle. On some bikes there is a sleeve at the mechanism end of the cable. You can adjust these sleeves by hand, unless they are mud-clogged or rusted tight. Loosen (c-cl) the lockring and then turn the sleeve counter-clockwise too, even though this may not seem right to you at first. It tightens the cable, because it has the effect of making the cable housing longer, which tightens up the brakes. Try out the brake. If it works OK now, tighten (cl) the lockring hard against the hand lever unit (not against the adjusting sleeve) and you're ready to go. If it's hard to tighten up the cable, try squeezing the brake shoes in against the rim with one hand while you use the other hand to fiddle with the adjusting sleeve; taking the tension off the cable often makes it easier to tighten the brakes. If you cannot get the cable tight enough even by turning the adjusting sleeve all the way out (c-cl), you have to do a major adjustment with the cable anchor bolt; turn the sleeve back in (cl) until it is at least halfway to its loosest setting, then tighten (cl) the lockring against the hand lever unit and go on to the next paragraph.

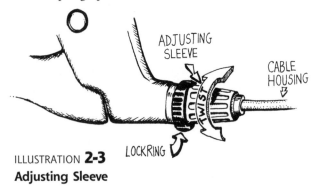

ILLUSTRATION **2-3**
Adjusting Sleeve

A *major brake adjustment* is hard to do on the road if you don't have two wrenches, or at least a wrench and a good pair of pliers, along with a friend who's willing to lend a strong hand or two so you can loosen and tighten the cable anchor bolt. Look at Illustration 2-4 and 2-5 to see where the anchor bolt is on your brake mechanism. First undo one end of the short transverse cable from its socket in the cantilever. Then get a wrench or the pliers fitted tight on the head of the anchor bolt. If you have a friend to hold the wrench or pliers on there good and tight, it makes the job a lot easier. While the anchor bolt is held still, turn the anchor bolt nut loose (c-cl) until the cable can slide through the anchor bolt. Then move the anchor bolt up the cable about a quarter of an inch (the anchor bolt is about a quarter inch thick, to give you an idea). You can gauge how far you are moving it by looking at the squished-flat section of the cable where the anchor bolt used to be. When you have moved the anchor bolt up, tighten (cl) the nut on the anchor bolt firmly, until you can see that it has actually flattened out the cable in the little hole. You should use both tools yourself to do the last hard tightening of the anchor bolt and nut. That way you won't twist the bolt out of your friend's hand. Hook up the short transverse cable and try out the brake. If it is a bit tight or loose, adjust it with the sleeve at the hand lever end of the cable as described in the *minor adjustment* section above.

On some brake systems, the main brake cable passes through the carrier and is anchored on the opposite cantilever from the one with the socket that you can pull the short cable's end out of, as shown in Illustration 2-4. If you are working on this kind of brake system, you have to loosen the anchor bolt *and* the little pincher bolt in the carrier. Do your tightening of the cable, then adjust the position of the carrier so the length of the cables to the two cantilevers is equal. This is a pain, but the system is safer.

If a *cable is broken*, the best thing to do is make sure the other brake is adjusted well enough to work, then ride home with extreme caution and replace the broken cable with a new one. If you have brought along a spare cable, just undo the anchor bolt on the old one, take it out, thread the new one in, and tighten it up as described in the *major brake adjustment* procedure earlier in this section.

If both cables are broken you have to figure out some way to use the rear one on your front brake. First look at the broken end of the rear cable. Is the break near the mechanism end? If so, and if the break is a pretty clean one, all you have to do is take the cables out of their housings and put the rear cable in the front brake system. Make sure you get the little ball or barrel at the end of the cable set firmly in its notch in the hand lever, then thread the cable through the little ferrules and the housing on down to the front brake mechanism. If the cable end is too frayed to go through the housing, you have to find your way to a farmer or somebody who has a pair of good wire cutters to clip off the frayed end. When you have a good clean cut on the end of the cable, thread it in.

Tighten your makeshift front brake as in the *major brake adjustment* procedure earlier in this section. If you have extra cable left over, wind it up in a little coil and tie the coil with the end so it'll stay out of the works as you ride cautiously home. Tie up or undo the rear brake's transverse cable so it won't flop down, catch a nobby, and slam on the rear brake. Do a complete recabling of both your brakes when you get home, using new, unfrayed cables. See a shop manual if you need more info.

Cable sticking. If you ascertained, by the diagnostic method in the OVERALL BRAKE SYSTEM DIAGNOSIS section for the brakes, that your cable is sticking, it's probably because the cable is either rusty, mud clogged, or kinked.

If the cable is rusty or mud clogged, you can grab the carrier with one hand and the hand lever with the other and just pull the thing back and forth a whole bunch of times; with luck, you'll loosen up enough of the crud inside the cable housing and ferrules so that the cable can do its job. If you have some lubricant, apply it at the places where the cable disappears into the housing and work it in as you horse the cable back and forth.

If the cable housing has a kink (a sharp, unnatural bend in the springy plastic-covered tube that the cable runs through), all you have to do is get a firm bare-handed grip on the housing on either side of the kink and straighten it. If the kink is at one end of the housing, like right next to the hand lever, make a mental note to loosen and remove the cable when you get home, then snip off the bent end of the housing, thread the cable back in, and reset the brakes. Don't try this out on the trail unless you have a good pair of cable clippers along. You may not be able to get the brake back together if the end of the cable is frayed. If this is the case, just straighten the kink as well as you can with your bare hands and ride home to your cable-cutting tool.

Brake Mechanism

PROBLEMS: *One-shoe drag*. One of the brake shoes refuses to come off the rim of your wheel when you release the brakes. First check to make sure the wheel isn't loose and cockeyed. Then check the brake mechanism. Usually all you have to do is pull the dragging shoe off the rim as far as you can, hold it there, and shove the carrier in the opposite direction, until it makes a new bend in the transverse cable. If the carrier is the kind that the main cable passes through, as shown in Illustration 2-4, you have to loosen the little pinch bolt in the carrier, adjust the position of the carrier so the brakes center, then retighten the pinch bolt.

If the springs on the two sides of the brake are out of balance, fiddling with the transverse cable won't solve the one-shoe drag; you have to adjust the springs. On some

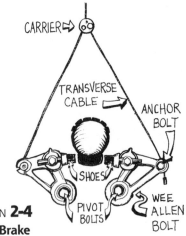

ILLUSTRATION **2-4**
Cantilever Brake

CARRIER

TRANSVERSE CABLE

ANCHOR BOLT

SHOES

PIVOT BOLTS

WEE ALLEN BOLT

brakes, there is a wee allen bolt that you can adjust to center the brakes. On some cantilever units, such as the Dia Compe 986 set, there is a pivot bolt that you can put an allen key into, and a thin adjusting nut between the body of the cantilever and the bike frame. Fit a cone wrench or the thin jaws of a Cool Tool on this adjusting nut. Loosen (c-cl) the pivot bolt with your allen key, then reset the position of the adjusting nut so the brakes are centered. Hold the nut in that position while you tighten (cl) the pivot bolt with the allen key. On some cantilever brakes, you have to undo the transverse cable to loosen the brake, then loosen (c-cl) the pivot bolt about five turns, grasp the whole cantilever unit and slip it out on the pivot bolt, until the end of the spring comes out of its little hole in the brake mount plate, then turn the cantilever so the spring end moves up to the next higher hole in the mount plate (there are usually three little holes, and you can often hook the spring in a notch at the top of the plate for one more extra-tight setting). Setting the spring tension this way is a pain; if you have a lot of trouble keeping your brake shoes centered, I recommend you switch to ones that are easy to adjust, like the Dia Compe 986 ones.

Stickies. If the brake shoes are slow to grab the rim and slow to release it, and the handle and cable are both OK, then the mechanism must be rusty, mud-clogged, or broken inside. If you can get some lubricant, put some on the pivot bolts. Then try grabbing a cantilever with each hand and rocking them back and forth a bunch. Take the wheel off the bike and repeat the cantilever-rocking action if you need to. (Just don't push so hard on them that you break the springs or the mechanisms.) Try loosening , adjusting,

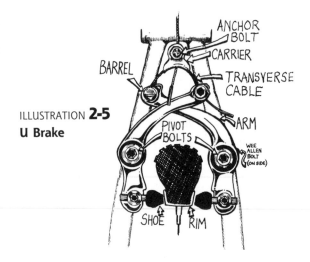

ILLUSTRATION **2-5**
U Brake

and tightening the pivot bolt, as described in the *One-shoe drag* section above. When you have the brake working passably, ride home and do a complete overhaul there, using a shop manual if you need help on the details.

Brake shoe cockeyed. You banged your brake or it rattled loose, so one of the brake shoes hits the rim cross-wise or not at all. Fix it immediately, before it wears a hole in the tire or gets stuck in the spokes. All you have to do is loosen (c-cl) the little bolt that holds the shoe to the rest of the mechanism (if it isn't already loose), then move the brake shoe around until you can see that it's lined up so it will squeeze exactly on the middle of the rim. It should look like the one on the other side, so the two grab the rim at the same angle. When you get it lined up, hold it there firmly with one hand while you tighten (cl) the mounting bolt. Take it easy on that bolt; some of them strip easily.

Brake shoes worn. If your brakes don't seem to work well and the shoes are worn down, don't panic. Worn brake shoes can often work as well or better than new ones if the brake system is adjusted and you use the brakes wisely. The first step to fix the brakes is to adjust them, as described in the *Cables* section above.

If your brakes are slipping because they are wet, all you have to do is *think ahead* about your braking, and put the brakes on lightly for a few seconds to whisk the water off both the rim and the brake shoes, so the brakes will stop you when you need them. This technique will almost always keep the brakes from slipping and then grabbing in that terrifying way that wet brakes do.

If your brakes are slipping from overuse and overheating on long, hot, steep descents, use them *intermittently* so they don't get so hot and glazed. If the hill is so steep that you need to use the brakes almost all the time, alternate your use of the front and rear brakes. You may have to stop and let them cool, or cool the rims off in the water at a creek crossing. Whatever you do, avoid the nervous tendency to leave both brakes on lightly as you descend. That just burns them up.

If your brake shoes are worn all the way down to bare metal, see if there is a rubber ledge that protrudes under the edge of the rim when you put the brakes on. If there is a ledge like that, take a pocket knife and cut the thinnest outer edge of it off. Then loosen (c-cl) the bolt that holds the shoe to the brake mechanism and shift the shoe alignment up so the new braking surface you have just made hits the middle of the rim. Tighten (cl) the mounting bolt while holding the brake shoe in its new position. Try out the

ILLUSTRATION **2-6**
Brake Shoe

brake to see if you have increased your stopping power. It won't be up to snuff, but it'll get you home if you take it easy. Install new brake shoes before your next ride.

Brake shoes squeaking or juddering. When you apply the brakes, your whole bike vibrates, and, if you're going fast, your brakes screech like a Model T with its original equipment. Don't let this bother you as long as the brakes stop you smoothly. If they are so juddery you can't make controlled stops, first check to make sure the cantilevers are mounted tightly to the frame. If your front brake is juddering badly, check the headset to make sure the bearings are adjusted right. Then check the brake shoe alignment. Get your head over the brakes and peer down past the tire at each shoe as you apply and release the brakes. Does the back end of either rubber brake shoe hit the rim before the front end? If it does, it may squeal or judder. On many cantilever brakes, you can loosen the mounting bolt and adjust the toe-in as well as the vertical and horizontal alignment of the brake shoe. You may have to twist a beveled (wedge-shaped) washer around the brake shoe mounting bolt, or shift the mounting bolt and some cupped washers to toe the shoe in more or less. If you can't get the brake shoes toed in right with gentle efforts, don't fight them. Use the brakes sparingly to reduce your squeaking or judder problem on your way home. Then you may need to change the shoes, cantilevers, or (if a front wheel is juddering badly) even the fork to solve your problem. Front wheel judder or fork flutter can be due to a combination of poorly aligned brake shoes, anodized or grutty/glazed rims, and a fork with too much fore-and-aft flexibility built into it.

3
Handlebars & Stem

DIAGNOSIS: For some reason, people often get confused about just what holds what in place on the handlebars and stem. The following symptoms tell you what part of the set-up is loose. If the handlebars swivel up and down, your problem is a *loose binder bolt*. If the bars are loose in relation to the front wheel, so they tend to aim off to one side or the other when you are riding straight ahead, the problem is a *loose or cockeyed stem*. If you have a bar end that is loose, all you have to do is line up the loose bar end with the other one, then tighten (cl) the mounting bolt that squeezes the bar end around the end of your handlebar, or the expander that goes in the end of the bar. If your handlebars are too high or too low, this also requires working on the stem, not the headset, as you might suspect.

No matter what you're doing to either your handlebars or stem, check to see that the tips of the handlebars or bar ends are plugged. If they aren't, plug them immediately, before you get back on the bike and start riding. If you don't have official bar plugs with you, use a wine or champagne cork, or even a short piece of stick with the end rounded off. Bare bar tips can be lethal in an accident. They can gore you if you fall on them.

PROBLEMS: *Binder bolt loose.* Tighten (cl) the nut on the bolt, or tighten (cl) the bolt with an allen wrench (usually 5 or 6 mm). Some beefy stems have two or even four binder bolts; tighten (cl) them all evenly, turning each a bit at a time. If your stem has only one bolt, and it spins when you tighten the nut on it, the little key or "dog" under the head of the bolt must be sheared off; all you can do is ride to the nearest farm or country garage with tools and borrow a pair of vise grips or strong pliers, then try to get a grip on the head of the bolt and tighten (cl) the nut as well as you can to get home. Then replace the bolt with a good strong one from a bike shop and use a box-end wrench on it rather than your adjustable wrench, so you get it good and tight.

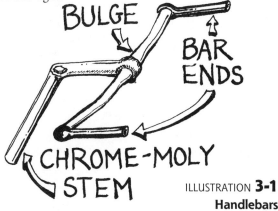

ILLUSTRATION **3-1**
Handlebars

If your bars slip because they are simply too small in diameter for your stem, loosen (c-cl) the binder bolt as much as possible, then find a smooth, uncrumpled aluminum beer or soda pop can (all too easy to find, on many backroads and trails). Cut out a 3-inch by 2½-inch strip of the side of the can with a sharp knife, being careful to keep the metal smooth. Use the strip you cut out as a shim,

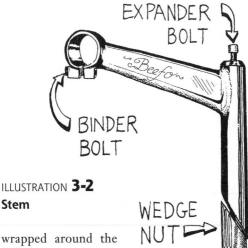

EXPANDER BOLT

BINDER BOLT

ILLUSTRATION **3-2**
Stem

WEDGE NUT

wrapped around the
bulged central portion
of the bars where they fit inside the stem. Tighten (cl) the
binder bolt as well as you can, and when you get home,
replace the bars or stem to get a better fit.

Loose or cockeyed stem. To straighten bars that have gotten cockeyed, stand in front of the bike and hold the front
wheel between your legs (you don't have to get weird with
it, just hold it still). Grasp the handlebars firmly with both
hands and straighten them so the stem extension lines up
with the front wheel and the bars run straight across. If the
bars won't budge, loosen (c-cl) the expander bolt, using an
allen wrench, then tap the head of the bolt with a hammer
or rock, to unwedge the stem so it can be straightened.

Once your stem and handlebars are straight, tighten (cl)
the stem expander bolt enough so the stem will stay put,
but no tighter. Try twisting the bars again. If they stay put
unless you pull quite hard to one side, the expander bolt is

tight enough. It should not be so tight that the stem can't slip in case of a crash. If you fall on the bars, you want *them* to give, not you.

Stem creaky, cracked, or broken. When you ride up hills and pull hard on the handlebars, your stem creaks. First check to see that it isn't loose; if it is, tighten (cl) the expander bolt as described in the previous section. Then check for cracks on the stem, and look closely to see if it is the correct diameter; it should just barely slip down into the fork column in the headset. If you find any signs of cracks on the stem, especially at a joint or near the binder bolt, ride home gingerly, without pulling or leaning down hard on the bars. If your stem is broken, undo the front brake (undo the transverse cable so it won't catch on the nobbies), tie or balance the bars on what's left of the stem, then ride home holding the stump of the stem, pulling on the rear brake cable where it runs bare along the top tube in order to stop. If you have no exposed section of cable running to your rear brake, you have to steer with one hand on the stem stump while you squeeze the brake lever with the other hand. Verrry tricky. Proceed with due caution.

Handlebars too high or low. To adjust the height of the handlebars, you have to loosen (c-cl) the expander bolt a couple of turns with an allen wrench, then tap on the head of the bolt with something heavy like a rock or a hard piece of wood. When the expander bolt is unwedged, undo the front brake transverse cable, then lower or raise the handlebars. Tighten (cl) the expander bolt as explained in *loose or cockeyed stem,* above. Then readjust the brakes as explained in the Brake Cables PROBLEMS section, and ride in comfort.

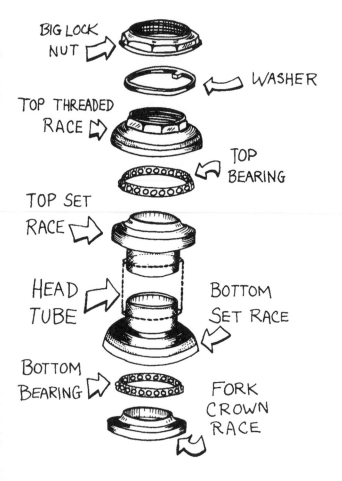

BIG LOCK NUT

WASHER

TOP THREADED RACE

TOP BEARING

TOP SET RACE

HEAD TUBE

BOTTOM SET RACE

BOTTOM BEARING

FORK CROWN RACE

ILLUSTRATION **4-1**
Headset

4
Headset

DESCRIPTION AND DIAGNOSIS: The headset is the set of bearings that holds your front fork to the rest of the bike frame and allows the front wheel to steer. The steering column at the top of the fork goes up through the head tube of the frame, and all of those bearing parts (see Illustration 4-1) of the headset go around the fork tube. There may be some variation of parts on your headset, such as a special lockring with allen set-screws, or seals on the bearing races, or interlocking teeth on the washer and the top threaded race, but the general layout will be the same. If your steering action gets unresponsive, or you hear clanks or grackly crunchy noises and feel looseness in your front end as you go over bumps, your headset is probably loose. Lift the front wheel off the ground a few inches and drop it; if you hear a clank, the headset is definitely loose. To test for more subtle headset looseness, apply the front brake fully, push down on the handlebars, and rock the bike forward and back. Can you feel a sort of slippy-shifty looseness or see that the front fork is shifting back and forth in relation to the frame? These symptoms indicate a loose headset too. Just to make sure the problem is with the headset and not the wheel, rest the front wheel on the ground and try to wiggle the tire from side to side; if the wheel wiggles, you may have loose front wheel bearings or a wheel that is loose in the fork. For either of these problems, see Hub PROBLEMS. If your steering action becomes rough or sticky, and you notice that the bike is a little hard to balance when you are going slow, the problem is probably that the headset is stiff.

PROBLEMS: *Headset loose.* If you have noticed a clanky or wandering front end and used the diagnostic tests above to determine that your headset is loose, here is the way to snug it up. First, see if you can turn the big top locknut counter-clockwise a turn or two to loosen it. Try doing it by hand. If it has allen setscrews set into the sides of it, holding it tightly in place, loosen (c-cl) those with an allen key (assuming you have one that fits along with you), then loosen (c-cl) the locknut.

After you have loosened the locknut, tighten (cl) the top threaded race by hand. If the headset is loose, you should be able to do this easily. You can often do it even if you couldn't manage to loosen the locknut; however, if the washer and the top threaded race have little intermeshing teeth all around them, you must work that top locknut loose at least three turns before you can tighten the threaded race.

When you have the threaded race as tightly as possible, apply the front brake and rock the bike back and forth to see if there's still any looseness. If so, tighten the threaded race some more, rocking the bike to and fro, or turning the handlebars as you tighten, to make sure you are snugging up the race on the bearings as much as possible.

When the headset is snug, tighten (cl) the locknut down by hand too. If you just happen to have the proper wrench for your headset locknut (Cool Tool makes little attachments for the different size headsets) tighten the locknut thoroughly. If you don't have a tool, just hand tighten the locknut. That will hold it there for a while. If you go over a lot of rough terrain, you may have to retighten the headset by hand again before you get home.

When you do get home, don't forget to adjust the headset carefully again, then tighten the locknut thoroughly with the proper wrench. Also, if the headset is an aluminum one, you might want to replace it with a steel headset. Aluminum headsets have a reputation for looseness.

Headset stiff. Either the bearings are dry or tight, or the steering column may be bent. Look at the front end of the bike from one side. Does the front wheel look cocked back further than it should be? Have you slammed into a log or rock lately? Taken a bad endo (flipped over the front)? Try steering the handlebars all the way to the right as far as they will go, and then all the way to the left. If the headset gets stiffer at either extreme, you can almost bet you have a bent steering column. This is hard to straighten, but if the bend is severe and steering is really bad, see page 39 for a way to get the fork pulled out straight.

If the steering column is straight and the only problem is that the bearings are dry or dirty, get a bit of lubricant worked into the headset. Turn the bike upside down and squirt the lubricant in, using the little application tube if it comes with one. If the bearings aren't sealed, it's easier to lube them; I remember squeezing mayonnaise from one of those little packets you get at fast food places into my headset once. Worked like a charm. But if you do any stop-gap lubrication on a ride, make a mental note to do a complete overhaul of your headset when you get home, using proper bike grease and a shop manual to make sure you get it all right.

If the headset is just too tight, you have to try to loosen (c-cl) the top locknut, then loosen (c-cl) the top threaded race just a bit (one eighth of a turn or less), then tighten (cl) the top locknut. You need a headset spanner to do this properly; the one you get with a Cool Tool will work if the top locknut isn't really tight. If it is really tight, you may have to struggle along with your stiff steering until you can get to a farm or something, and borrow a big adjustable wrench to loosen and tighten your top locknut. Do adjust that tight headset as soon as you can, though; a tight headset feels horrible when you try to correct imbalance by steering, especially when you're picking your way through a slow, technical section of trail. If you don't believe this, just try riding no-handed with a tight headset.

5
Frame & Fork

DIAGNOSIS: If you completely crumple any of the tubes of your frame, or if a joint breaks when you are out in the middle of the wilderness, you can't do much about it. If the bike is still rideable, ride it very gently; if not, walk. There are *some* tricks you can use, like, if a fork blade breaks, whittle a stick down to the right diameter, then jam it into one end of the blade and push the other end of the blade over the other end of the stick. But such repairs are rarely workable. Prevention works better; try to get a really durable frame, and respect its limitations by using good technique going over obstacles. Good frames don't usually break unless you are riding foolishly. One frame and fork problem that can happen to anybody, though, is a bent-in front end. And fortunately, there are things you can do to try to straighten it out.

PROBLEMS: *Front end bent in.* So you hit a boulder. Or was it a log? Or was it that dip at the bottom of the gully that you thought you could pull the front end up out of, but you didn't quite make it? Oh yes, it can happen to any of us, and *has* happened to many of us. The result is that either your fork or your down and top tubes are bent, or all three are bent, and now your wheel hits the down tube so you can't ride home.

Try this last-ditch method of straightening the front end of your bike a bit; it won't make the bike perfect by any means, but it may get you home. My thanks to cyclo-crosser Dan Nall for this trick; he showed me how to do it when we were *way* out in the woods, and this guy from Topanga "lunched out" in a rocky creek bed.

Have a friend hold the bike upright, or prop it against a post or a tree, and sit down on the ground with the front wheel between your thighs. Push the pedals around with your toes until the right crank (the one with the chain-wheels) is pointing down and the left crank is pointing up. Place your left foot on the chainwheel, with your heel against the right crank, and place your right foot against the bottom bracket shell, with your toes up along the left crank, as shown in Illustration 5-1.

Now grab either the ends of the fork or the rim of the wheel where it is nearest to your chest. The taller you are, the easier it'll be to pull on the rim. If you are less than five feet tall you may have to take the front wheel off so you can pull on the drop-outs at the ends of the fork.

When you have a good grip on the rim or fork, straighten your back (you'll strain it if it's curved) and try to hold the fork or wheel absolutely still as you push the bottom bracket and the rest of the bike away from you with your feet. Make your legs do the work, not your back and arms. If you have a light, unreinforced frame and fork, you may be amazed at how easily you can pull the front end of the bike out. Some super-heavy-duty frames and forks may be impossible to straighten using this method.

If your fork is the only thing that is bent, and you have a really sturdy front end on your frame, you can try another straightening method; it is primitive, but if you are stuck out in the middle of nowhere, you may want to try it anyway. All you have to do is turn the front wheel all the way around backwards (you may have to undo the front brake and loosen the stem to do this), then put the front wheel against a tree and shove the bike from behind. Easy does it. I saw a desperate racer try this method once, only he sorta hurled the bike down on its reversed front wheel, and instead of neatly straightening his front fork, he neatly crumpled both his top and down tubes, which neatly took him out of the race, since the nearest spare bike was about five miles away.

There are other ways to pull a front end out, like wedging the forks in the crotch of a tree and levering the frame back, but I think these methods have much more potential for ruining the bike than fixing it.

Whatever you do to straighten things out, don't keep using your bent and straightened fork or frame. When you have limped home,

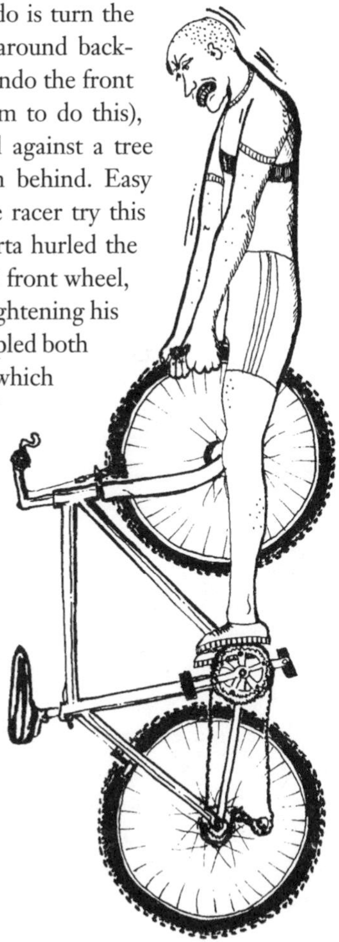

ILLUSTRATION **5-1**
Pulling out the front end

take the fork or the whole frame to a first-rate bike shop and see if it can be accurately straightened by a pro framemaker, or if it should be replaced. And next time, use a bit more finesse to get over those rocks, logs, and holes at the bottoms of gullies.

Fork Flutter. When you put on the front brakes as you are flying down a bumpy single-track, the front end of your bike starts to waggle and jerk fore-and-aft under you. If you glance down (don't stare; you are flying down a hill, remember), you can see the fork flexing or fluttering fore-and-aft. The flutter takes on a rhythm all its own, which can throw off your judgment of obstacles ahead, and even throw you into an endo (over the bars), if the hill is steep and you have to put the brake on hard. The problem is a bad wave of vibration repeating itself in the fork. The harmonics from hell. They are caused by brake shoe judder and/or bouncing over bumps, amplified by anodized or crud-crusted rims; certain combinations of fork type and frame geometry can make flutter more of a problem. In my experience, round, thin-gauge, wide-diameter, straight steel fork blades, with a short offset and a fairly steep head angle are more susceptible to flutter than other types of forks. But I have heard of small-diameter, curved-blade forks fluttering too. The cheap solution to the problem is to toe in your brake shoes (see *brake shoes squealing or juddering* in the Brakes chapter). If that and cleaning or sanding your rims don't help, you have to ride home carefully, taking it easy on the bumpy downhills, then buy a different fork.

6
Wheels & Tires

DESCRIPTION AND DIAGNOSIS: The wheel is the whole round thing you roll on. The tire is the rubber part of the wheel that fits on the rim. I know that sounds obvious, but you can still hear lots of people say their "tire" is loose, when their wheel is loose.

The most common problem you'll have with your wheels is flat tires. To fix a flat, go to the *flat* section under Tires. If you don't have a flat, but your *tire is soft*, refer to the section by that name.

If your wheel is loose or if it's making grindy-crackly noises, see Hubs PROBLEMS. Don't ride with a loose or grindy hub or you may ruin the bearings or even the whole wheel.

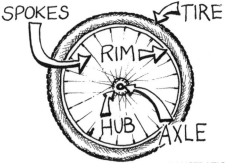

ILLUSTRATION **6-1**
Wheel Parts

43

If your wheel is bent and wobbly, but it will still spin around OK, ride it home and either take it off and take it to a pro to be "trued" or do the job yourself when you've got lots of time and a good book or teacher to make sure you do more good than damage to those delicate spokes and rims. If you're stuck out in the sticks with a badly bent wheel and have to get it unbent enough to ride home, see *bent rim*.

Tires

PROBLEMS: *Flat.* Bah. You got a flat. Well, don't let it get you down. Cyclists have been fixing them for a long time. Follow the procedure below, and you'll soon be on your way. If you do the repair well and keep the tire well inflated, chances are it will be a long time before you get another flat; Mountain Bikes are much less flat-prone than most other bikes. Unless, of course, you live in the thorny Southwest, in which case you might want to put some flat-proofing solution in your tubes.

Flats are due to either slow leaks, quick leaks, or blow-outs. No matter what kind of a flat you have, *don't ride the bike on a flat tire! Not even on a soft tire!* You can ruin both the tire and the rim of the wheel. If you don't have a pump or patch kit along, you can make a last ditch effort by pulling one bead of your tire off the rim, packing your tire with dry leaves or grass (the dried stems of tall grasses like wild oats seem to work best), and pushing the rim back onto the tire; this trick, from the pages of *Mountain Bike Action* magazine, can help you plod your way out of the woods in an emergency. It's better to repair the leak and ride home with air in the tire, however, so if you have a patch kit and pump, just settle down under the nearest shady tree and go to work on the following procedure.

First check the valve if you suspect that it might be the cause. Pump up the tire. Spit on your fingertip and put it lightly over the end of the valve. Tilt your finger tip a wee bit so the only thing between it and the valve end is the spit (on a presta valve, the kind with the tiny metal screw-down cap, you have to use two moist fingers to make this test). If little bubbles come through the spit, your valve stem is leaky. Try pushing the stem in and releasing it a few times (loosen the tiny metal cap first, if you have a presta valve). If that doesn't help and you happen to have a first aid kit with pointed tweezers in it, you can stick the points of the tweezers down in the valve and tighten the stem in there. If you have one of those pronged valve caps like the one shown in Illustration 6-2 you can use that even more easily. If you can't fix your leaky valve, you have to go through

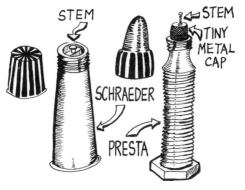

ILLUSTRATION **6-2**
Two different tire valves

the wheel and tire removal procedure below, then put in your spare tube. If you have no spare tube, you have to pump the tire up and ride as fast as you can until the air leaks out again; if the valve isn't really shot you can usually ride a half hour or so between pump-ups.

If the valve is OK, but you can hear air hissing out of the tire someplace, find the leak, and if you see the cause (a thorn or piece of glass or whatever), pull the cause out and throw it far from the trail. Make a mark on the tire where the hole is with a pen or pencil or make a little scratch in the dirt on the side of the tire or on the rubber tread using a stick or your fingernail.

If you have only one small hole in your tire, and you have a patch kit, you can patch the tube without taking the wheel off the bike. Just lay the bike down on its side and turn the wheel until the part of the tire with the hole is out where you can get at it easily. Then skip down to the section about getting the tire off one side of the rim.

Patching or replacing a badly punctured tube requires a series of steps. First you hang the bike up, then you remove the wheel, get the tire off, and deal with the punctured tube. Then you put the patched tube or a new tube back in the tire and get the tire back on the rim, and finally you put the wheel back on the bike. The whole procedure takes some time and patience. If you don't get too harried about it, though, you can usually get going again in about ten minutes.

For a start, find something to hang the bike up on, like a fence post or a low tree limb. A sturdy bush or a stalwart friend will do. If you have an extra inner tube (don't use the one you'll need to replace your leaky tube) you can tie it around the seat tube and sling it over a tree branch; an inventive guy named Cliff Binkley gave me that idea; he hangs his bike from his ceiling using old inner tubes. The bike doesn't have to be held up that high, just high enough so the end of it with the flat tire is a few inches off the ground.

The next thing to do is look at what's holding the wheel to the bike. There will be big nuts on the threaded ends of the axle, or a little quick-release lever on the left side of the wheel.

If you have a flat on a front wheel, all you have to do is loosen (c-cl) the nuts or pull the quick-release lever out, away from the center of the wheel, and the wheel will slip out of the front fork; the flat tire should slide right past the cantilever brakes, but if it doesn't undo the transverse cable from one of the arms, so the brakes open wide.

If you have a rear wheel flat (and they're much more common), don't loosen the axle nuts or the quick-release lever just yet. First get the bike in its highest gear. That means getting the chain onto the smallest sprocket on the freewheel. When you're in high gear, loosen the axle nuts or quick-release lever. Then squat behind the bike, put your left hand on the rim of the wheel where it is nearest to you, and with your right hand grab the body of the rear gear changer or "derailleur."

Push the wheel forward and down with your left hand as you pull the gear changer and chain back toward you. This action, combined with a gentle jiggling of the wheel, will get the rear sprocket free of the chain. Keep the jiggling to a minimum, so the chain doesn't get tangled up or yanked off the front sprockets as well as the back ones. If the tire hangs up on the cantilever brakes, pull the barrel-end of the short transverse cable out of its slot on one of the cantilever arms, so the cantilevers open up wide.

Once you've got the wheel off the bike (or in a good position to fix the puncture, if you only have one small puncture), you have to get the tire at least part way off the rim. First push in the little stem tip on the tire valve (on presta valves, loosen the tiny cap before you push the stem tip in) so you get all the remaining air out of the tube. Run your fingers all the way around the tire, squeezing and pinching the beads (edges) in to loosen them if they're stuck to the rim. This will give you an idea of how tough it's going to be to slip the bead of the tire off the rim. If the tire is quite loose, all you have to do is grab a section of the bead with both hands and pull away from the center of the wheel, so one bead of the tire stretches up, as shown in Illustration 6-3. Lift that stretched-up place over the rim, then work your way around the wheel, spreading the section of bead that has been pulled over the rim. If you are fixing a single puncture with the wheel still on the bike, you only have to pull about one quarter of the tire bead off the rim; enough to get in there and pull out the section of the tube that has the puncture.

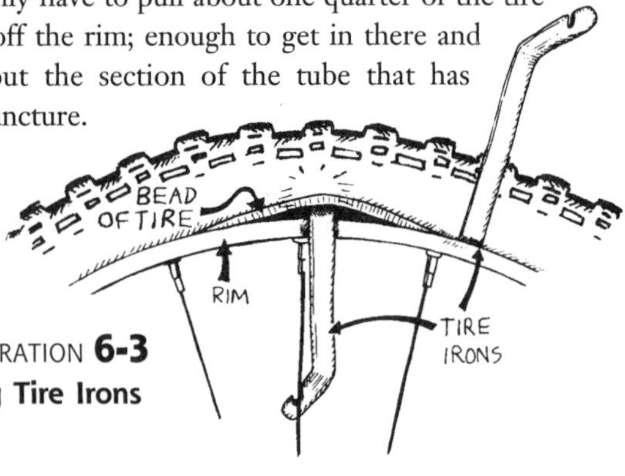

BEAD OF TIRE

RIM

TIRE IRONS

ILLUSTRATION **6-3**
Using Tire Irons

If the tire is a tight, high-pressure one and you can't pull a section of the bead over the rim by hand, use your tire irons. Do *not* use a screwdriver or any other substitute. Stick the round, spatula-shaped end of your tire iron a little way under one of the beads of the tire. Nudge the sidewall of the tire in with your fingers to make sure the iron doesn't grab on the tube, or go under both beads of the tire and pinch the tube between them. Pinching the tube can easily put a new hole in it, even if you are using proper tire irons. When you have the iron under just one bead of the tire, pry all the way out and down, then hook the handle end on a spoke, as in Illustration 6-3.

With a second iron, pry out more of the bead, a couple of inches along the bead from where you made your first pry. If you need to make a third pry and have only two irons, hold the bead outside the rim with your thumb, then pull the second iron out gently, move it a couple inches, and do another pry. Usually two pries will get the tire bead well on its way.

When the bead is on its way (when it doesn't try to jump back onto the rim), take the tire irons out, stick one iron between the popped-out bead and the rim, and peel the rest of the bead out of the rim, just like you'd pare a giant potato; of course, if you have the wheel on the bike still, you can only peel off the bead about a quarter of the way. Don't take any more off the rim than you have to; that just makes more work putting it back on.

To find the leak, pull as much of tube out of the tire as you can, but leave the valve in place. Pump up the tube until it swells to about two times its normal size. If the thing won't hold any air at all, the leak must be a really bad one, and easy to find. You'll probably have to replace the tube in this case. If the tube does fill up, look for the leak. You may have to move your ear around the tube, listening for it, or even pass the tube close to your eye to feel the air against the delicate surface of your eyeball. Some pinpoint leaks are hard to spot. Don't wet the tube if you can avoid it; those bubbles from a leak are easy to spot, but the wet tube must be dried *completely* before patching.

When you do find the leak, mark it so you don't forget where it is. If you have a little pen or crayon in your patch kit, make arrows or "cross-hairs" pointing at the leak from about one inch away on each side, as shown in Illustration 6-4. If you have no marker, use the sandpaper in your patch kit to "rough up" a 1-inch area of the tube, making sure your leak stays in the exact center of this rough area.

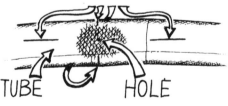

CROSS HAIR MARKS

TUBE   HOLE

ILLUSTRATION **6-4**
Roughing up the tube

Figure out what kind of hole it is and what made it. Find out *now*, before you forget. There's nothing worse than getting two flats from the same cause. If the hole is a small round one, look for a nail, staple, thorn, or thin shard of glass embedded in the tire casing. If you line the tube up with the tire, it's usually easy to find the culprit. If the hole is a small gash, there will probably be a bigger slash in the casing of the tire. If the tire slash is over ¼ inch long, you have to put a "boot" under it when you put the new or repaired tube back in. If you have no boot in your tire kit, you can rig up one from various sturdy, flat objects; I've seen tire boots made out of folded-up swatches of sandpaper, dollar bills, double-layered duct tape, and even a Power Bar (not just the wrapper, the *whole thing*).

If the hole in the tube is too big to repair and you don't have a spare, you can cut or tear the tire in half at the hole, then tie the two ends together in a tight knot. Pump up the tube to make sure the knot is air tight. It's hard to stretch this shortened tube back over the rim, and it can be hard to get the tire back on the rim if it's a tight-fit tire, but if you're really stuck with no alternatives, you can usually get the tire to work, and bump-a-lump your way home rather than walking. Thanks to the wrecking crew at *Mountain Bike Action* magazine for this bit of trailside wizardry.

If the hole is on the inner side of the tube, look for a sharp spoke end poking through the rim strip. If there are two tiny holes on the inner curve of the tube (they're often called "snake bites"), they are probably due to the rim and tire bead pinching the tube when you went over a curb or other angled obstacle; your tire was under-inflated, and when you went over that bump, the shock of the blow made the tire bead chomp down on the tube.

Remove any puncture-causing debris you find stuck in the tire casing. Run your finger gently around the inside of the casing while you're at it. This will root out any sources of further flats before they happen. If the rim is rough (like at its joint) near the point where you have snake bite punctures, use your swatch of sandpaper to smooth out that roughness.

If there's a sharp spoke end sticking up, pull the rim strip away from it, set your screwdriver tip on one side of the spoke end, and whack the screwdriver with a rock or something, as if you were hitting a chisel with a hammer. The idea is to bend the nasty spoke end over, or, if the spoke end is short, to chip it right off. If it's too short to bend over or snap off, file it as smooth as you can with your sandpaper from your patch kit, then put a little wad of rag or paper or a spare tube patch over the thing, so it can't poke through the rim strip and into the tube again. Make a mental note to take the spoke out and replace it with one that's the right length when you get home.

When you have found and removed or filed down the cause of your tube leak, hold your finger over the hole in the tube, pump the thing up again, and listen and look your way around it once more, to make sure there isn't a secondary leak. When you're sure you've found and marked all the leaks and taken care of what caused them, deflate the tube completely.

If you have the wheel off the bike and want to take the tube out to replace or fix it, pull a six-inch section of the tire bead *that you already took out of the rim* back over the tube at the valve location. This will leave the tube free to be pulled directly away from the center of the wheel, thus slipping the valve straight out of its hole in the rim. With a presta valve you may have to unscrew a little nut or ring around the threaded stem before you can pull the valve out of the hole in the rim. If you have a spare tube and want to replace your punctured one, just skip the next few paragraphs and go on to the section on how to remount the clincher tube and tire.

If you don't have a spare, or if your spare already has a leak, and you have a small hole, like ⅛ inch in diameter or less, you can patch it. Some bike shops refuse to patch any tube with a leak. They just put in new tubes. Haughtily they quote Webster, who states that a patch is a "temporary repair." They pronounce that in their shop, only permanent repairs are done. They have a pretty good point, but if you have only one spare and you get two punctures, and you are miles from the nearest bike shop, you may not give a big damn about the temporary nature of the tire patch. What in the world *isn't* temporary, you might ask.

Clean and dry the tube around the hole, and rough up the surface with your piece of rough sandpaper if you haven't already done that. Make sure the hole stays at the center of the roughed up area, so you can center a patch of glue around the hole, and then stick the patch on with the hole in the center of it, too. The roughing and gluing often hide the hole, so it's best to have those arrows pointing to the hole from outside the scene of action.

If you've never done any patching before, you might want to practice the critical spreading of that thin patch of glue on some other part of the tube where there's no hole. Put the glue on quickly and lightly. Make a smooth, even, thin film of the stuff, larger in area than the size of the patch, but not much larger. Don't squirt out big blobs of glue, either; they don't dry completely. If you hold the lip of the glue container flush against the surface of the tube, then tip up one edge just a bit, you can spread the glue smoothly and evenly into that nice thin film; if necessary, rub the blobs smooth very quickly and lightly with a *clean* finger tip. If you do it right, it will look wet and shiny for a few seconds, and then turn a dull matte texture as it dries. Don't blow on it to make it dry quicker. If you spit or blow damp, misty breath on it, the patch won't stick as well.

If you did a trial glue area, put some dust over it (so it won't stick to the rim and the tire), then go back to the roughed up area around the puncture and do the real thing, to perfection.

Wait a couple of minutes for the glue to dry completely. Make sure no water or dust gets on it. Then take out the patch and eyeball the size to make sure it's going to fit inside the glued area. If you need to apply more glue, do so. Then take the little tinfoil or paper cover off the sticky side of the patch, being careful to keep your fingers off the sticky stuff as much as possible. If there's a thin piece of cellophane on the nonsticky side of the patch, leave it there so you have something to hold and something to push against when the patch is in place. If there isn't any cellophane on the patch, or if the cellophane wants to peel off rather than the tinfoil cover, just hold the very edge of the patch with one fingernail while you peel the cover off the rest of the sticky side. If you have several punctures and run out of patches, you can use a piece of duct tape as a patch; just wrap it around the tube, not too tightly, and proceed as normal.

Stick the patch in place, making sure it lies down smoothly, without ripples or bumps. Then pinch and knead the patched tube between your fingers, starting at

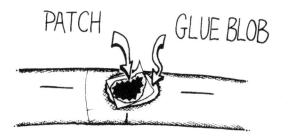

PATCH   GLUE BLOB

ILLUSTRATION **6-5**
Applying the patch

the center of the patch and working out to the edges. Squeeze it as hard as you can, maybe stacking up the first fingers and thumbs of both hands to double your squeezing power. Make extra sure it's tight along the little lines or seams on the tube; those seams can make little channels for the air to seep out of if the patch isn't gripping really tight on them. Some people like to use the back end of their pumps or the back sides of the curved end of a plastic tire iron to press down the patch; whatever works for you.

When you're sure the patch is on there to stay, and stuck well all around the edges, take a little fine dust and poof it around the patch, so the extra glue that's still showing will get a light coating on it. That way it won't stick to the inside of the tire or the wheel.

Your patched tube is ready for use immediately. Make one last check before you remount it, though; pump the tube up to about one and a half times its normal size. Run your eye and ear around the tube to make sure it doesn't have any more holes or a leaky stem.

To remount the tube and tire, start by letting almost all the air out of the tube. If you are putting on a brand new tube, pump a bit of air into it so it isn't flat and unmanageable. Find the hole in the rim for the valve and push the free bead of the tire at that point all the way over the rim until you can see the valve hole. Poke the valve in there, then pull the free bead back over the tube. Working away from the valve in both directions, stuff the tube up into the tire and tuck it into the rim, out of sight and out of your way. If you have to put in a boot to cover a slash in the tire, do it now.

Work the remaining tire bead over the lip of the rim with your thumbs, making sure the tube doesn't get twisted or pinched between the tire bead and the rim. When you get down to the last few inches of the tire bead, it will get tough, especially if you have a tight-fitting tire. Roll up your sleeves. Focus your energy. And make sure the tube is deflated almost completely and tucked in there out of your way, so you don't pinch it and put a new hole in it. If you can find some "dry lube" like really fine dust or ashes, poof some of it on that last section of the tire bead to help it slide over the rim. Even a dab of spit on the bead may help you get it on.

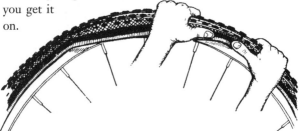

ILLUSTRATION **6-6**
Pushing the tire bead on

Most mountain bike tires aren't that hard to mount, but if you have a tough, tight-fitting one, you'll need all the help you can get. Work with both thumbs on one section of the bead, as shown in Illustration 6-6. Don't try to pop the whole thing over the rim at once until you have only a couple of inches to go. It takes a lot of oomph on those thumbs; you can hold one part of the bead in place, as the right hand is doing in the illustration, and roll the rest of the bead into place with the palm or heel of your free hand. Just don't slam the wheel around in your excitement—they bend easily. And *don't* use a screwdriver, or, if you can possibly avoid it, even a tire iron. Anything you stick under the tire at this juncture could reach in there, snatch the tube, and pinch a hole in it.

Just get the bead on a bit at a time. Franz Kafka once wrote, "There is only one human sin—impatience." Not that you can be expected to keep your patience when the tire bites your finger, then jumps off the rim, allowing the tube to flap out at you like a kid sticking out his tongue. Don't throw the wheel in your anger; they bend, remember.

When you get the bead onto the rim, go back to the valve and push it in and out of the rim a couple of times, wiggling the tire between your fingers as you do so, to make sure the tube isn't pinched between the tire bead and the rim right next to the valve. If it is, you'll make an awful thump-thump-thump going down the trail. When the tire and tube are seated in the rim as they should be, have a swig of water, relax a bit, then come back and pump the tire up.

If the tire goes flat, do the wet finger test on the valve. If the valve doesn't leak, it must be another hole in the tube.

Call the tire, tube, wheel, and whole bicycle what they are, and start all over. I know exactly how you feel.

If the tube holds air, slap yourself on the back, have another relaxing swig or two, and (if you took the wheel off the bike) go on to the procedure for replacing the wheel on the bike.

Replacing the repaired wheel is simple if it is a front one. Just make sure the quick-release lever or big axle nuts are loose, then slide the wheel into the forks and tighten (cl) the nuts or push the lever tight (on the left side, of course), checking to see that the rim is centered between the brake shoes as you do the tightening up. If you had to undo the brakes to get the tire in or out, push the brake shoes into the rim with one hand and slip the loose end of the transverse cable back into its notch in the cantilever. You're ready to ride.

Replacing a rear wheel is a bit more of a trick. First make sure the axle nuts are loose or the quick-release lever is in its wide open position. On many bikes, it's even necessary to hold the lever with one hand and the cone thingy on the other side of the wheel with the other, so you can loosen (c-cl) the quick-release to make room for slipping the wheel back into place. If the brakes are tight and it was hard to get the wheel out between them, undo the transverse cable from one cantilever to release the brakes.

Now get in the squat-behind-the-bike position you assumed to pull the wheel out of the frame. Hold the wheel in your left hand, as you did before, and grab the gear changer mechanism with the other. Pull the changer back a bit, so the chain doesn't sag so much. Then jockey the wheel into place in front of the changer, so the upper span of the chain goes over your smallest rear sprocket. Move the wheel up and back into its slots (dropouts) in the frame. If it hangs up on its way into the slots, have a friend fuss with the quick-release or the nuts and washers or the brakes or whatever is causing the hangup. Just keep one hand on the changer and the other on the wheel so you can move the wheel gently into place.

Slide it as far back as it will go, then line up the tire so it is centered between the chainstays, up forward near the bottom bracket. If you have vertical dropouts, lining up the wheel correctly is a cinch. Now you can move your right hand from the changer up to the wheel where it's centered, like the guy has done in Illustration 6-7. Keep the wheel exactly centered there while you use your left hand to tighten the quick-release lever on the other side of the wheel. Tighten (cl) both big axle nuts thoroughly with your adjustable wrench if you have axle nuts instead of a quick-release lever.

ILLUSTRATION **6-7**

Tightening rear wheel in place

If you had to undo the brakes to get the tire in or out, push the brake shoes into the rim with one hand and slip the loose end of the transverse cable back into its notch in the cantilever. When everything is back together, take a little ride around to make sure the brakes, gears, and newly inflated tire all work. If they do, feel free to whoop with delight, and have good time on the rest of your ride. Keep an eye out for sharp thorns and broken glass, though...

Tire soft. This may be due to a slow leak or the natural seepage of air out of a tube over a long period of time. If you have any suspicion at all that your tire is too soft, make the following foolproof test. You can use a tire gauge instead, but frankly, it won't tell you as accurately what the right tire pressure is *for you.*

To make an *edge test*, find a rock or tree root with a relatively sharp edge; something that will serve as a sort of stair edge. Roll the tire in question up onto the edge, as if the bike is climbing up the "stair." Push down on the bike from above the wheel and watch the tire at the point where it is resting on the edge of the rock or whatever. What you are doing here is imitating what happens when you ride over a sharp-edged obstacle. The edge should flare out the tire, but only a little bit, even if you push down hard and suddenly. The tire should not give so much that you feel the edge clunk against the rim. On the other hand, the tire should not be so hard that there is no flare-out at all when you push down; fat tires are supposed to absorb the thousands of natural shocks that mountain bikers are heir to, after all. If you do the edge test on a tire and the edge clunks against your rim, pinching the tire and tube, you need to pump up your tire. If you don't pump it up, you'll waste a lot of energy fighting the rolling resistance of those soft tires, and you'll risk getting a snake-bite puncture, as well. Now, some riders like to vary their tire pressure depending on the terrain, hard for pavement, softer for off-road; that's fine, as long as the tire hardness is within the range that passes the edge test.

Get a pump or CO_2 inflater that fits well on your type of valve; if you are riding with several other folks who have pumps, find the one that works best on your tire; the better the pump works, the less time the whole group will have to wait for you to pump up.

You will probably be using a frame pump or mini-pump, the kind with the connector right on the end of the pump. You have to make sure you can hold the pump and the bike wheel steady while you pump, so you don't tear the valve off in your efforts to inflate the tire. Lean the bike against a tree, fence post, or boulder, and turn the wheel until the

ILLUSTRATION **6-8**
Edge test

valve is at such a height that you can brace the pump against your left knee while you pump with your right hand. Hold your left hand with your thumb cocked against the rim if you have to for extra stability (left handers, just reverse all those rights and lefts).

The point of this odd posturing and thumb cocking is to keep the pump from jumping and tipping around in relation to the tire valve. Check to make sure the tire is seated

ILLUSTRATION **6-9**
Pumping up

WHEEL
BRACED
ON TREE

THUMB
BRACED
ON WHEEL

ELBOW
BRACED
ON KNEE

PUMP

well in the rim as you pump it up; the bead should be sunk down into the rim evenly, all the way around. If part of the bead is bulging up and out of the rim, *stop* pumping, let all the air out, and work the bead down all around the rim with your fingers to get it all settled into place. Then you can go back to pumping. Do the edge test now and then to see if you have the tire pumped up enough. If you have a small pump and big tires, it will take a fair amount of pumping, but mountain bike tires don't have to be pumped up to a hundred pounds per square inch, so it shouldn't take you long. When the tire feels hard, do a quick edge test again to make sure you are in the permissible range of hardness. Then ride in peace. You have just fixed the root of about half the hardships people ever have with their bikes! If you master the flat, and learn to keep oil on your chain, you are pretty much the master of your mount.

Hubs

DESCRIPTION: The hub is the thing in the center of the wheel that holds the bearings.

PROBLEMS: *Wheel loose or noisy.* Either your wheel feels loose and unsteady under you, or it rubs constantly against the brakes or frame, or the thing makes cracky-grackly noises. Do what you can to fix it, *now.* You may need more tools to do a good overhaul and adjustment at home, but try to get it halfway functional so you can ride home without losing a wheel or destroying the bearings.

If the wheel is noisy, try to squirt a little lubricant into the bearings if they aren't sealed. If they are sealed or if you don't have any lubricant, just ride home directly and do a complete overhaul there.

If looseness is the problem, first see if the wheel is loose in the frame. If you wiggle the wheel with your fingers, does the axle slop around in relation to the dropout slot in the frame? If so, tighten (cl) your big axle nuts or your quick-release lever, *now*. Losing a wheel on a downhill is a major mess.

If you have a quick-release lever and it isn't holding the wheel firmly even when the lever is pushed all the way in, first try swinging the lever around to the other direction to make sure you are pushing it to its tight position and not to the loose extreme.

Is the quick-release lever loose no matter which way you push it? OK, you have to tighten the unit up. Aim the lever straight out, then grab the little round cone-shaped nut at the other end of the quick-release skewer (on the other side of the wheel). Hold the round nut still with one hand and turn the lever end of the skewer clockwise a half turn or so. Then push the lever to its tight position and see if it holds the wheel firmly in place. If the lever is still loose, pull it out straight and turn it (cl) again while holding the round nut. It should be pretty hard to lock the lever into its tight position, so the wheel can't jiggle loose.

There are some super-light, quick-release lever units out there that require a last little turn *after* you lock the lever into its tight position. If you have such lever units, turn the lever clockwise to tighten it after locking. This is needed most on rear wheels with non-vertical drop-outs. Personally, I think a lever unit is inadequate if you have to turn it after locking; I'd use it to get home, but then I'd replace it with a slightly heavier but functional quick-release lever. You wanna save that weight in a better way? Figure out the optimum height for your seat, put the seat there, and replace the quick-release lever on your seat post with a lighter unit, a simple binderbolt. So there.

If your wheel still wiggles when the big axle nuts or quick-release lever are tight, your problem is loose cones. It's hard, and sometimes impossible, to get the cones adjusted right without official Hub Spanners like the ones on page 13. Sometimes you can use a Cool Tool and a regular adjustable wrench, though, so if your bearings are really loose and you have those tools, try to follow the procedure below.

Before you fiddle around with the bearing unit, first take a close look at it, and at Illustration 6-10, to identify all the parts. You can't see as much of them on your bike as you can in the picture, and at the end of your axle you'll have either a big axle nut or a quick-release lever that partially hides the other stuff, but peer behind and around the obstructions and wipe off any grime and grease in there, so you can see the parts, which appear in this order: first a big nut or quick-release lever, then the dropout of the frame, then a thin locknut, then a washer, and then a cylindrical cone, which disappears into the hub and which has two slots at its outside edge for a thin spanner.

ILLUSTRATION **6-10**
Hub, Exploded view

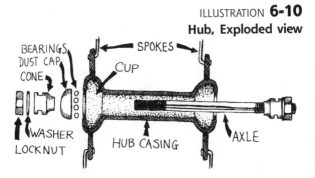

Know what the parts are on your hub now? Great. The procedure for adjusting the cones will be different depending on whether you have quick-release levers or not, and depending on whether it's a front or rear wheel you're working on. Find the paragraph below that applies to you and go to it.

If you have a front wheel with big axle nuts, tighten one of them so the wheel will stay in place, and loosen the other. Then reach behind the dropout with a thin-jawed wrench, such as a hub spanner or the adjustable wrench on a Cool Tool. Get the jaws of the tool onto the slots of the cone and turn it clockwise until it is snug on the bearings. If the locknut is not tight against the cone and washer, you can even snug the cone in with your fingers. Back the cone off a quarter turn or less, then tighten (cl) the locknut against the cone and tighten (cl) the big axle nut on that end of the axle, too. See if the wheel can spin smoothly. If the bearings are too tight, you have to loosen (c-cl) all the nuts and stuff outside the cone, then loosen the cone (c-cl) a bit, then tighten (cl) everything back up again.

If you have a front wheel with a quick-release lever, pull the lever out and take the wheel off the bike, then see if either cone-and-locknut set is still tight against itself, so the parts can't be turned around the axle. Put a regular adjustable wrench on the locknut of the tight set. Adjust the wrench carefully so it fits tight on the flats of the locknut (some locknuts have slots so you have to use a thin-jawed wrench instead). Tighten (cl) the cone on the other side with your fingers, or a thin-jawed wrench such as a hub spanner or the adjustable wrench on a Cool Tool. Just snug the cone up on the bearings, then back it off a quarter turn or less. Tighten (cl) the locknut against the washer and cone, using your thin-jawed wrench, and holding the other end of the axle still with a regular adjustable wrench. Then take the regular adjustable wrench off that locknut, and while you hold the cone still with the thin-jawed wrench, tighten (cl) the nearby locknut against it with the adjustable wrench. Then take all wrenches off the bearing parts, grab the locknuts and the ends of the axle with your fingers, and give the wheel a spin. If it rolls easily without slopping around on the bearings too much, put the wheel back on the bike and get riding. If the bearings are too tight, you have to loosen (c-cl) the locknut you just tightened, loosen (c-cl) the cone a bit more, then tighten (cl) the locknut again.

If you have a rear wheel with big axle nuts, tighten (cl) the axle nut on the right side of the bike. Next loosen (c-cl) the big axle nut on the left side, where there aren't any sprockets and gear changers in your way. Then use a thin-jawed wrench such as a hub spanner or the adjustable wrench on a Cool Tool to first loosen (c-cl) the left side locknut, then snug (cl) the cone in against the bearings. Back the cone off a quarter turn or less, then tighten (cl) the locknut against the cone and tighten the axle nut so the whole wheel is held firmly in place again. Give the wheel a spin. If it rolls OK without a lot of slop, ride on it. If the bearings are tight now, loosen (c-cl) the nuts on the left end of the axle again, then loosen (c-cl) the cone a bit more, then tighten (cl) those other nuts again.

If you have a quick-release rear wheel, put the bike in its highest gear, so the chain is on the smallest sprocket, then take the wheel off the bike. See page 47 if you want some hints on this. When you have the wheel off, put your adjustable wrench on the locknut that is the only part of the bearing unit showing on the right side of the hub, just visible in the middle of all the sprockets. Adjust the wrench carefully so it fits tight on the flats of the locknut (some locknuts have slots so you have to use a thin-jawed wrench instead). Then reach around to the other side of the hub and use a thin-jawed wrench such as a hub spanner or the adjustable wrench on a Cool Tool to tighten (cl) the left cone until it is snug against the bearings. Back it off (c-cl) a quarter turn or so, then tighten (cl) the locknut against the washer and cone. Then take the adjustable wrench off the locknut on the sprocket side of the wheel and use it to tighten (cl) the other locknut firmly against the washer and the cone you adjusted, holding that cone still with your thin-jawed wrench. After doing this final tighten-up, take all wrenches off the bearing parts, grab the locknuts and the ends of the axle with your fingers, and give the wheel a spin. If it rolls easily without slopping around on the bearings, put the wheel back on the bike and ride. If the bearings are too tight, you have to loosen (c-cl) the locknut, loosen (c-cl) the cone a bit more, then tighten (cl) the locknut again. When you remount the adjusted wheel, make sure the quick-release lever is holding it very firmly in place. If it isn't see page 64 for the method to tighten up the quick-release mechanism.

Spokes and Rims

DESCRIPTION: The rim is the thin aluminum hoop that your tire fits on. Spokes are the lacy wires that keep the rim round. They do it by pulling evenly, all the way around the wheel. At the rim end of each spoke there is a nipple that can be turned tighter or looser to increase or decrease the tension on the spoke so it pulls evenly with its fellow spokes. The rim and spokes of a wheel weigh about two pounds. They withstand forces that boggle the imagination every time you fly over a jump or slam into a large rock. Needless to say, spokes can break and rims can bend. It is miraculous that they don't get broken and bent more often.

PROBLEMS: *Wheel bent or wobbling.* You hit a bad bump, or went into a rut, and one of your wheels is no longer round. It's no fun to ride on a bent wheel, but if you can get home on it, do so. Truing a wheel properly is a high art. If you want to do it yourself, practice the art in peaceful, unpressured surroundings, with a good book to help you (see the Appendix). Or take the job to a pro.

If, however, you are out on the road and have a wheel that's so bent it won't get you home, here are some things you can try in order to get it rolling.

If the wheel is hitting on the brakes, but not the frame, loosen the brakes with the adjusting barrel, as shown in Illustration 2-1. This will mean you have to ride home with only one good brake, so ride cautiously.

If the rim is sprung out of round, so the wheel looks like a potato chip (some people say it's pretzeled, others say tacoed; pick your bent-food expression) and the tire slams from one side to the other if you try to turn the wheel, hitting the brakes and all the frame stays, you've got to resort to drastic methods if you're going to be able to ride home at all.

First look at the wheel from above it to get an idea of just how bad the bends are and how many there are. If the whole wheel has been reduced to a cupped-hand shape, so that, for instance, the tire valve and the rim joint opposite the valve are stuck out to the right side of the bike, while the sections of the rim halfway between those points are both bent out to the left side, you have a classic example of a sprung wheel. If only one short section of the wheel is bent out to one side from the center, with perhaps two small sections bent the other way, one on either side of the main bend, you have a one-point-impact bend. They are usually easier to fix up enough to ride on; if you have a one-point bend, skip the sprung wheel melodrama below, and go on to the single bend straightening procedure, three paragraphs down.

A sprung wheel may well be hopeless. But true boonie bikers never give up hope until they are forced to. So here's a last-ditch wheel-saving trick you can try. You've got nothing to lose, as long as you don't get so rough you crack the wheel hub.

Take the wheel off the bike (see page 47 if you need advice on this) and let a little air out of the tire if it is pumped up really hard, like 60 pounds of pressure or more. Then find a tree or post or boulder that has a root or small rock sticking up about a foot out from the base. What you want are two solid objects to brace the opposing sides of the rim against, as shown in Illustration 6-11. If either bracing point is a rock, pad it with some cloth or a spare tire or something, so you don't bend the rim even more than you have already. You can even use a short log braced against a tree for your lower wheel bracing point. Be creative. Set things up so you have the wheel resting against something solid at the top and the bottom.

Now, the points of the rim that should be braced are the ones that are bent farthest *away* from you; the points are bent toward the tree or rock, in other words. If the top and bottom of the wheel are bent toward you, just rotate the wheel ninety degrees so the bends are going the right way.

Put the heels of your hands on the parts of the rim that are bent closest to you. If these points are near the bottom bracing point, rotate the wheel a half turn, so they are nearer to the *top* of the wheel. When your hands are placed correctly, give a shove, leaning the weight of your weight into it. Push gently a couple of times to get the feel of things, then harder once, a good, sharp shove. This should

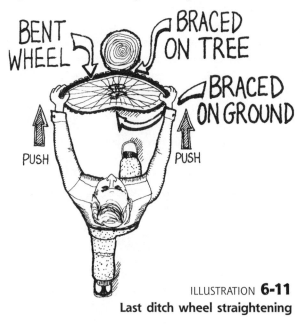

BENT WHEEL

BRACED ON TREE

BRACED ON GROUND

PUSH   PUSH

ILLUSTRATION **6-11**
Last ditch wheel straightening

bend the wheel considerably if you really put your body into the shove. Sometimes the wheel pops back into a shape that's almost round. If it goes round, then pops back into a potato chip shape, try again, just a wee bit harder, but not so hard that you spring it the other way. Sometimes, especially with narrow rims, the wheel will suddenly spring into a shape that's surprisingly close to straight. If this happens, don't argue with success. Pump up the tire a bit if it's really soft, but keep the pressure on the low side. Then wrap any broken spokes around their neighbors to keep them out of trouble, and ride home with a song in your heart, but go easy. When you get home, you can try to do a real truing job, with the help of a shop manual, or better yet, replace the rim, or just take the wheel to a pro.

If one of the bends comes out of the wheel when you shove on it, but you still have a single bend left over, or a bend and a couple of secondary bends going the other way, fix them according to the method that follows.

If you have a single bend from a run-in with a big rock, or one big bend with a couple little ones going the other way on either side, first see if you can get the wheel somewhere nearer to straight by using a variation on the last ditch effort shown in Illustration 6-11. Turn the wheel so the big bend is at the top of the wheel, *bowing away from you*. If there are mini-bends, they will now be at either side of the big bend, and curving toward you.

Let a little air out of the tire if it is pumped up really hard, then lean the big bend against your upper bracing object. Make sure the bracing object is padded if it's a rock, then put the heels of your hands on either side of the big bend (right on the secondary bends, if the wheel has them) and give a short, sharp shove. Don't heave your whole body into the shove unless you weigh less than 120 pounds. The idea is to shove with your arms until you feel the metal of the rim give just a bit. The wheel may go almost straight the first time you shove, or it may take three or four little shoves. Don't push too hard in any case; you don't want to bend it the other way, or spring the whole wheel into a potato chip.

When the wheel is roughly round, so it can at least spin without hitting the frame, you can loosen your brakes and ride it home, then do a good truing job on it, or take it to a pro.

If you have a spoke wrench, lots of time and patience, and a gentle touch with things mechanical, you can try to get it pretty close to true by adjusting the spokes, so you can leave your brakes tight and go on riding. Truing a wheel out in the boonies only makes sense if you have a long way to ride to a bike shop, though, and if you have any broken spokes, you usually can't get the wheel close to true without some spare spokes.

Before you start wildly twiddling with the spokes, first make sure the tire isn't rock hard, then spin the wheel and look closely at the rim as it goes past the brake shoes. Look for "blips" as well as wobbles. A blip is a little outward flare or bump in the rim, caused by hitting a sharp object like the edge of a rock or a curb. Your brakes will grab on this blip, causing skids and tire wear. But you need a special tool, a vise grip wrench, and a keen sense of how to use that tool, to fix a blip. Best to leave it for a shop, or ride home and fix the blip there with the proper tool and a good book that tells you how to use it. Out in the wilds you have to settle for fixing the wobbles.

To fix a *minor wobble*, first let some air out of the tire, if you haven't already. Next tighten the brakes, if the wobble isn't already hitting one brake shoe or the other. If you have a brake adjusting sleeve (see Illustration 2-3), use it. If you don't have one, find a chip of wood or a little stick, apply the brakes, then jam the wood chip into the gap that opens between the brake hand lever and the brake handle post (see Illustration 2-2) so the brake shoes are held in close where they'll touch the rim at the wobble.

Now, to get the wheel closer to straight, you want to move the section of the rim that's hitting the brake shoe away from it. This is done by alternately tightening and loosening a bunch of spokes. For instance, to move the rim to the *left*, *tighten* (cl) the nipples of the spokes that go to the *left* side of the hub and *loosen* (c-cl) the nipples of the spokes that go to the *right* side of the hub, as shown in Illustration 6-12.

As you tighten and loosen spoke nipples, keep a couple of things in mind. The ideal wheel has exactly the same amount of tension on every spoke. So, in your adjusting, don't leave any spoke completely loose, and don't tighten just one spoke in order to do all the work of moving the rim over. Think of a wobble as the result of a group of six or eight maladjusted spokes—not just one errant individual, but a misfit minority.

To move the rim laterally, you want to adjust the whole group of six or eight nipples. If any of the spokes in the group you are working on is obviously much too tight or much too loose, you have to try to bring it into the same range of tightness as the other spokes in the group.

BRAKE SHOES

WHEEL RIM

TURN

TURN

SPOKE TO RIGHT SIDE OF HUB

SPOKE TO LEFT SIDE OF HUB

RIM WOBBLES
TO THE RIGHT,
MOVE IT TO
THE LEFT

ILLUSTRATION **6-12**
Straightening a minor wobble

You have to pick up the "feel" of the median tension of all the spokes. One way to get that feel is to go around the whole wheel, tightening and loosening every spoke about a tenth of a turn. It takes a while, but it's a good warmup exercise, especially if you aren't a hot-shot wheel maker. You might find, right away, that all or most of the nipples are rusty and frozen tight to the spokes, so they're very hard to turn at all. If your wheel has a lot of frozen nipples (a very uncomfortable condition, I'm sure), use the last ditch straightening method on page 70 and try to get the wheel round enough to carry you home, then take it to a pro. If you try to fix it with your spoke wrench out on the trail, you'll probably just break a bunch of spokes or strip the flats off the nipples.

You might find that all or most of your spoke nipples are loose. Most likely, the factory or shop that put your bike together didn't tighten up the spokes enough, so the whole thing is coming apart on you. This is a really serious problem. You can make the wheel much worse by trying to tighten up the spokes, if you don't do the tightening just right, so the increasing tension stays even all around the wheel. The best solution is to just go around the wheel tightening every spoke with your bare fingers, then start at the tire valve and make one more trip around the rim, turning each spoke *exactly one half turn* with your spoke wrench. If the wheel is still real loose and wobbly, take another trip around the rim giving each spoke a half turn. But *don't* tighten the spokes more than a half turn at each trip around the rim! When the whole wheel seems pretty tight (each nipple takes a little oomph to tighten) go on with this straightening procedure and try to get the wheel round enough to get you home. Don't expect anything near perfection; hops, wobbles, and general egg-shapeness are likely, unless you have a natural knack at the art. Just make a mental note to take the wheel to a first-rate bike shop and have the wheel expert retrue it, as soon as possible.

Even if the spoke nipples turn OK and aren't all loose, you will find variations in the tension of the spokes. This is especially true of rear wheels. The rear wheels of most multi-speed bikes are flattened or "dished" to compensate for the sprockets being on one side. Look down on your rear wheel from above and you'll see how the spokes go out farther on the left than they do on the right. If the wheel is made just right, this won't mean that those right spokes are too tight, but in far too many cases, the right spokes have been cinched in extra tight to dish the wheel.

When you work on a rear wheel, you'll often find that half the spokes are much tighter than the others, and you have to accept their tightness when fixing a wobble. Even on a front wheel you may find some spokes have been over-tightened to make up for an imperfection in the rim.

The whole point is, don't try to make the wheel perfect. Just work to create a lateral movement of the bent portion of the rim, to straighten it enough so you can use it. And do this without putting too much or too little tension on any one spoke.

Twiddle the spokes at your wobble a bit at a time, loosening the ones to the same side of the hub as the wobble and tightening the spokes to the opposite side of the hub from the wobble, as in Illustration 6-12. Adjust the whole group of six or eight spokes, then check to see how much you've improved the wobble. Be careful you don't generate secondary wobbles on the ends of your original wobble. Tighten and loosen the spokes more in the middle of the wobble and do less tension adjustment near the ends of the wobble. If you get the wobble close enough to straight that the wheel will spin freely between the brake shoes, don't try to take things any further. Ride home and do a thorough job when you have more time, or take the wheel to a pro if you aren't satisfied with your slightly wobbly wheel. I don't mind having a little wobble or two in my rear wheel, because I never look back there; I'm pickier about front wheel wobbles because I have to look at the wheel as I'm grinding up a long grade.

If you begin to have trouble with your one big wobble turning into several frustrating small ones, and you begin to lose patience, *quit now*. Go get a drink of water, have a power bar, look at the scenery for a minute. Whatever it takes to calm down. If you don't, those spokes can start playing coyote tricks on you. Wobbles appear magically where moments before there was only straightness. One big gentle wobble turns into three sharp little ones; a totally new wobble appears on the other side of the wheel. That sort of thing. It can get like the scene in *Fantasia* with Mickey Mouse and the multiplying brooms.

With some experience, you will learn the elusive "feel" of spoke tension that controls all those secondary wobbles. But if you are new to the game, and stuck out in the wilds somewhere, just try to get the wheel round enough to carry you home.

If you have a pump or tire inflator, before you pump your tire up on your usably round wheel, check for spoke ends sticking up through the rim. Let all of the air out of your tire. Put a finger under the tire and run it around the rim strip. If there are spoke ends sticking up through the rim strip, or even poking big bumps up in the strip, take the wheel off the bike and take the tire off the wheel so you can take care of those sharp spoke ends, as explained in the *flat tire* procedure on page 44.

Broken spokes. These are most common for heavy riders who do not have heavy-duty rear wheels. If you bust a single spoke on a short ride, and the wheel doesn't have too bad a wobble because of it, or if you can use the method described in the previous section to get the wobble tolerably straight, just wrap the broken spoke around one of its neighbors to keep it from snagging on things and making weird noises, then ride home, where you can get a correct replacement for the spoke, and have the wheel fixed and trued by a pro; you can fix the thing yourself, but frankly, if you are heavy (over 200 pounds) and your wheel is not a heavy duty one, it's going to be hard for you to true your wheel well enough to prevent further spoke breakage.

If you break more than one spoke, and you are out in the middle of nowhere, and you have a long way to go to get to any bike shop with a hot-shot wheelsmith, and if you have some spare spokes, a spoke wrench, and (for rear wheel work) a freewheel remover or cassette cracker (all these things are described in the *Tools* section of Chapter 1), you can replace your broken spokes by yourself. The job can be a real pain, but you should do it, to prevent further spoke breakage and increasingly bad wheel wobbles. A really bad wheel wobble can ruin your brakes and even weaken the frame if the tire rubs badly.

First take the wheel off the bike and take the tire off the rim, as described on pages 47–49. Peel back the rim strip so you can see the spoke nipples of the broken spokes. Take the ends of the broken spokes out of the hub and the rim. If you are working on a rear wheel, chances are the broken spokes are on the side of the hub that's blocked by the cluster of sprockets on your freewheel or cassette. Agh. You have to limp out of the wilds and go to a bike shop for rear sprocket removal before you can remove the spokes.

When you have removed a broken spoke and its nipple from the wheel, take a new spoke in hand and line it up next to one that's already on the wheel to make sure it's the right length. If the head of the spoke is even with the hole in the hub, the other end of it, the one with the threads, should just reach the rim.

Push the new spoke into the hub so it goes through the hole in the same way the old one did. The spokes that go through the hub holes on either side should be the other way around. For instance, if the head of your spoke winds up on the outside of the hub flange, the two adjacent spokes should have their heads on the inside of the flange. Pull the new spoke through the maze of others, and get it so it's pointing straight out at the rim, without touching any of the other spokes. You may have to curve the spoke a little to get it woven through there, but that's OK as long as you don't put a sharp bend in it. A gently curved spoke will straighten out as you tighten it up.

When you have pulled the spoke all the way through, so its head is seated against the hub flange, it will not be pointing at the hole for it. To get it aimed at its proper hole, first look at the two spokes whose heads are on either side of the new one in the hub flange. These spokes will both run out to the rim in the same direction, either forward or back. The spokes must alternate, so if the two spokes on the sides of your new one go forward, make yours go back, or vice versa. Move your spoke end through its brothers, like a dancer weaving through a Virginia Reel, until it points at the hole in the rim. It should be able to barely stick into that hole, or at least come quite close to sticking into it.

Now check to see if the other spokes in the wheel are "laced." On almost all bikes, the spokes cross each other several times on the way out to the rim. On laced wheels (which all decent bikes have), the spokes touch at the point where they cross nearest to the rim. This is for lateral stability. If your wheel is laced, make sure you weave the new spoke through the old ones to match the lacing of the other spokes around the wheel.

Insert the nipple through the hole for your new, correctly laced spoke. Spin the nipple onto the spoke and tighten it with your fingers at first. Turn to page 56 so you can get your tire back on the rim and your wheel back on the bike. Then true the wheel, as explained on page 74, making sure the new spoke gets into the same range of tightness as the ones around it. That way the wheel won't be overstressed any more, and if you ride carefully, you probably won't break any more spokes on your way home.

Do a first rate truing job when you get home, or have a pro do it. If you are a heavy or hard-driving rider, get special heavy duty wheels made for you; mountain biking asks a lot of your spoked wheels. Make sure they are in the best possible shape for future rides.

7
Seat or Saddle

PROBLEMS: *Seat Loose.* If it *tilts forward and back* on the end of the seat post, get the allen wrench that fits the tightening bolt on the clamp that is at the top of the post, and tighten (cl) the bolt thoroughly. As you tighten, shift the seat slightly every once in a while to make sure it is settling into the right grooves in the mounting clamp.

If your *seat swivels from side to side*, or the whole post slides down into the frame tube so the seat is too low, you have to tighten the quick-release or binderbolt that holds the seat post in the bike frame. First loosen the quick-release lever or loosen (c-cl) the binderbolt, then move the seat to the right height for you. I'm not going to tell you what that height should be, but generally, riders like the seat set at such a level that when they sit on it, they can put the pedal at the bottom of its stroke, stretch their leg out straight, and rest their heel flat on the pedal. Much higher, and you have to rock your fanny to pedal; much lower and your knees have to bend too much at the top of each pedal

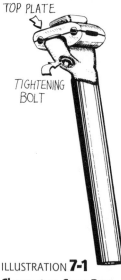

TOP PLATE

TIGHTENING BOLT

ILLUSTRATION **7-1**
Clamp-top Seat Post

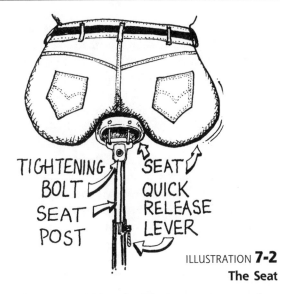

TIGHTENING BOLT

SEAT QUICK RELEASE LEVER

SEAT POST

ILLUSTRATION **7-2**
The Seat

stroke. Measure pedal length with *your* seater centered on the bike seat so that as you pedal along the trail *your* seater doesn't rock from side to side on the bike seat, creating saddle sores.

When you get the seat where you want it, look down on the seat from above and make sure it is pointing straight ahead, so the tip of it is lined up with the top tube of the bike, then tighten (cl) the binderbolt, or hold the lever end of the quick-release unit and tighten (cl) the cone end a half turn or so, then clamp the lever down all the way. Make sure the seat post is held firmly in place. Some seatpost binders require tightening one or more allen bolts. Others have hard-to-reach hex bolt heads. Get the tool that fits on your setup, be patient, and make sure you get that binder tight, one way or the other.

If no amount of patient tightening on the binderbolt will tighten the frame tube up enough to hold the seat post still, you must have a post that's too small for your frame tube. Not to worry. If you can find an aluminum beer or soda can, you can fix up your loose seat post in a jiffy. Just cut a rectangular piece of aluminum out of the side of the can, about 1 inch by 2½ inches in size. Use your pocket knife to do the cutting, and cut the edges as clean as possible, smoothing off any burrs or bumps along the edges by wrapping the piece of aluminum around your seat post, then rubbing the edges flat with the edge of the handle of your knife or something, then sanding the leftover burrs off with the little swatch of sandpaper from your tire patch kit.

The resultant curved, smooth-edged swatch of aluminum can be used as a "shim" to make your seat post wider. Just loosen the binderbolt or quick-release all the way, pull out the seat post, then wrap the shim around the seat post and slide the whole business down into the frame. If the frame is too tight, use your screwdriver to pry the top of the frame tube a bit wider apart. Slide the seat post and shim in carefully, so the shim doesn't get mashed out of shape. Adjust the seat height and get it pointing straight ahead, then you can tighten (cl) the binderbolt or the quick-release lever, and get on your way.

Seat hurts. Agh. This is a nasty problem, especially on a long ride. The short, cruel answer to it is that you should have taken several short rides to get tough before you took off on a long ride. But there are some things you can do to limit the agony if you are out on a long ride and have to get home somehow.

Make sure your pants are clean and as dry as possible where you sit, and that they don't get bunched up under there. Tight cycling shorts with a clean, soft liner in the crotch are best. If you don't have these, just do the best you can to keep your pants clean and smooth underneath you. Ever wonder why cowboys like often-washed, shrink-to-fit Levis? Now you know. But don't try wearing tight Levis on bike rides; the seams are in the right places for cowboy saddles, not bicycle saddles.

Adjust the bike seat so it's close to level and neither too high nor too low, then change your hand position on the handlebars as you ride, so you can sit in different places, forward and back on the seat, resting your weight on slightly different parts of that tender region of your anatomy. This is tough to do with standard flat handlebars; if you have bar ends, use them; if not, you can often ride smooth sections of trail or road with your hands turned upside down (palm up), or wrapped around the ends of the bars, or hanging on to the brake levers, so you can move a bit on the seat. Even just bending your elbows a lot as you ride downhill will change your body position enough to give your seater some relief.

When you get home, you might spend some of your recovery time looking for a new seat. Some people like the ones with extra padding bulges at the points where the two pelvic bones meet the seat. Others like the ones with little pockets of gel for their bony points. Whatever padding you get on a seat, though, make sure it is just at the points where your pelvis rests; the front portion of the seat needs to be narrow and virtually unpadded, so you don't chafe your upper thighs on it as you pedal. That rules out sheepskin seat covers. They're OK for very short trips to the market, but not for real mountain biking. And while we're talking tough, remember that the best prevention for a sore seater is not just having a good bike seat, but taking lots of short rides on it so *your* seater gets tough. OK?

8
Power Train

DESCRIPTION AND DIAGNOSIS: The power train is what should deliver your pedal power to the rear wheel. The front half of the system consists of the pedals, the cranks, the bottom bracket set, the front chainwheels (sprockets), and the front changer (derailleur). Between the front and back halves of the power train runs a messy, oily chain. The back half of the system consists of the rear sprockets (on a freewheel or cassette) and a rear changer (derailleur).

When you have a power train problem, first find out which half is acting up, then zero in on the individual part that's ailing and fix it. Don't just start fiddling with any part that comes to mind; you can spend hours trying to fix things that are OK before you start solving your actual problem.

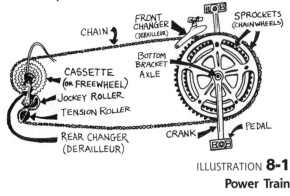

ILLUSTRATION **8-1**
Power Train

87

Here's a little trick to keep in mind no matter what your power train problem. If you can't solve the problem and you're out in the middle of nowhere, there is a way to get home on your powerless bike, as long as you have a cycling friend and a spare tube along. Simply loop your spare over your friend's seat post and hold onto it so he or she can tow you. If the two of you are about the same size or if you are larger, you should offer to do at least half of the towing work, and let your friend have the free ride. It's hard work on the uphills, but it sure beats walking. Aah, how thankful I have been for the help of Bryan, my backwoods cycling companion over the years. You're a true gentleman, Bryan, even if you did want to murder me that time I got us lost in Dead Man's Gulch.

Diagnosis of power train problems involves listening to the bike as you ride it. If there are nasty *grinding, rubbing, squeaking, kerchunking, clinking, or clunking noises* when you pedal, make this simple test: get going at a good clip on a quiet, level place or a slight downhill with smooth ground, then coast and listen. If the nasty noises do not stop when you stop pedaling, your problem is in a wheel, not the power train. See Wheel PROBLEMS and check for brake *stickies* (page 25) too.

If a nasty noise appears only when you pedal, see if it repeats itself, and how often. If it repeats once each time your pedal makes a revolution, then it's probably a front half problem. If it repeats itself approximately once for every two revolutions of your pedal, then you have a chain problem; go directly to Chain PROBLEMS on page 103. If the noise repeats two to three times for every revolution of the pedal, you probably have a back half problem; see

Rear Sprocket PROBLEMS (page 111) or Rear Changer PROBLEMS (page 125). If the noise you get is constant and unvarying, it might be any of the parts of the power train. Stop the bike, hang it up or have your friend hold it up, and listen to each part of the power train as you turn the pedals by hand. Two common steady noises are a squeaky chain and grindy rear changer rollers. When you have isolated the problem area, turn to the section that covers it so you can zero in on the specific trouble.

If your *gears slip* or change by themselves, there's something wrong with the control lever or cable adjustment. See *slippage or stickies* on page 112.

If the chain keeps flying off the front sprockets, or if the chain is always rubbing the front changer, see Front Changer PROBLEMS on page 122. On the other hand, if the chain keeps getting sucked into the space between the front sprockets and the chainstay, see Chain PROBLEMS on page 103.

If you hear a plunk-plunking noise when you're in a low gear and the chain is on the largest of the rear sprockets, STOP RIDING!!! That innocuous little sound is a warning that the rear changer (derailleur) is badly out of adjustment or alignment, and it is about to self-destruct in the rear wheel spokes. See *Changer System adjustment* on page 114 to save the mechanism from certain death.

9

Front Half of
Power Train

DIAGNOSIS: If you have a problem with the front half of your power train, you have to find out where it is, then go to the section about the ailing unit. If your chain is throwing or your front changer rubs on the chain all the time, however, just go straight to Front Changer PROBLEMS on page 122, with the rest of the stuff on changers. Also, if your chain is sucking all the time, see Chain PROBLEMS on page 105.

If your chain goes *kerchunk* and jumps up each time it hits a certain point of the front sprocket, see Front Sprocket PROBLEMS. If you hear nasty noises, like clicks, clunks, or harsh squeaks at each revolution of the pedal, first check the pedal itself. Is it hard to revolve on its spindle by hand? Is it real loose on the spindle? Is it obviously bent or bashed? When you spin it by hand, does it catch and stick on its bearings? Has the dust cap flown off, letting muck and dirt into the bearings? Look at Illustration 9-1 to get oriented, then see Pedals PROBLEMS.

If you hear a clunk, creak, or sharp squeak each time you push down on one pedal or the other, or if you sometimes feel a slight slippage of a pedal as you push hard on it, or if one of the cranks is knocking on the frame, see Cranks PROBLEMS. If you fix the cranks and still hear a squeak,

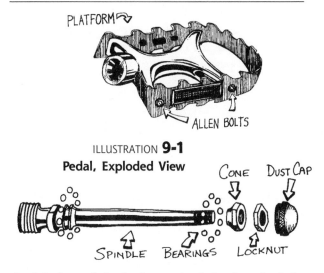

PLATFORM

ALLEN BOLTS

ILLUSTRATION **9-1**
Pedal, Exploded View

CONE   DUST CAP

SPINDLE   BEARINGS   LOCKNUT

check for loose chainwheel mounting bolts, then check the
pedal to see if it has come loose in the crank, then check the
pedal bearings, then check the bottom bracket bearings.
Sometimes front half squeaks are hard to chase down.

If you hear grinding noises that you can't pin down on
the pedals, or if your whole front half can slip back and
forth and wiggle in the frame, or if the whole front half is
hard to turn, see Bottom Bracket PROBLEMS.

Pedals

PROBLEMS: *Pedals loose or tight and noisy.* First make
sure the spindle is screwed tightly into the crank. If it's
loose, you need to get a wrench that'll fit tight on those two
flats that are on the spindle right next to where it screws
into the crank; the Cool Tool adjustable wrench will do the
trick, though it doesn't give you much leverage; the same is

true of a 15 mm hub spanner. Keep in mind, as you tighten, that the left pedal has left-hand threads, which means that you turn the spindle *counter-clockwise* to tighten it. Tighten the right pedal spindle clockwise, like normal threaded parts. If you can't get a loose pedal really tight, just keep an eye on it as you ride home, then get an official pedal spanner and really honk on it for maximum tightness (just don't overdo it and strip those aluminum threads out of the crank).

If your pedal is hard to turn, or makes noise when you turn it, check the bearings. If the pedal has a dust cap over the outer end of the spindle, see if it has an allen wrench hole, or see if it is loose enough to take off with your hands or a pair of wide pliers, if there is no allen wrench hole. When you get the dust cap off, look inside. Do you see the end of the spindle and a nut that's threaded onto it? That means the bearings are adjustable. Or is there a sealed bearing (a black ring-shaped thing) with no nut in sight? That means you have sealed, nonadjustable bearings, and they are shot. All you can do is ride home and get a shop to replace them.

If the bearings are adjustable, and you can wiggle the pedal back and forth on the spindle, back off (c-cl) the locknut on the end of the spindle by sticking your adjustable wrench jaws in there end-wise. Many pedals don't give you enough room to get in there; you may want to just oil the bearings and ride home to take on the adjustment hassle there. If you decide to adjust them on the trail, you have to undo (c-cl) the allen bolts holding the platform to the pedal and remove the platform. Then tighten (cl) the cone by sticking a screwdriver in along the outer wall of the bearing housing and then sliding it around (cl) until it catches on one of the flats of the cone and tightens it. Then tighten (cl) the locknut. Put a drop of oil in there and try to get a drop into the bearings at the other end of the pedal, too. If the pedal is tight (hard to turn), adjust the cone (c-cl) to make it a little looser. As with all bearings, these should be set so there is very little "play" or wiggle-room; just enough to let the little balls roll around freely. When the bearings are adjusted right, tighten (cl) the dust cap in again, put the platform on again if you took it off, and you're ready to go.

Pedal bent, bashed, or broken. You have to limp home or to a bike shop as best as you can. In many cases you can use the other foot to do the work of pedaling, and just give the mashed pedal a light push as it is going down, in order to get your usable pedal back up to the top of its stroke so you can heave down on it again. If you make it to a shop, see if they'll lend you a spanner to remove the shot pedal by unscrewing (c-cl on the right pedal, cl on the left) it. Make sure the threaded end of the new pedal is the right size, and that the threads are of the same type as those on your old pedal. Pedals from some countries don't fit in cranks from other countries. Tighten (cl on the right pedal, c-cl on the left) the new pedal in thoroughly, and you're on your way.

Cranks

PROBLEMS: *Clunk, creak, or sharp squeak* heard at each revolution of the pedal. You may not even hear any sound, but still feel slippage each time you push down hard on one of the pedals. Either symptom probably indicates that your *crank is loose* where it attaches to the thick axle that goes through the bottom bracket in the frame. Don't ride the bike with a loose crank! You need a socket tool or a crank bolt tightening tool to tighten up your crank; if you have a Cool Tool, the socket tool in it will fit most crank bolts. If you don't have a tool for your crank bolt, hobble to the nearest farm shop (amazing how many of them now have metric tools for their Japanese tractors), garage, or bike shop. Use only the tight crank to pedal. Don't use the loose crank to pedal hard, especially up steep hills. You can easily mess up the crank so much you'll have to buy a new one.

When you have a crank tightening tool, do the following test to make sure you have a crank problem, and to determine which crank is loose. Get off the bike and lean it against a tree or something, then position the pedals so one is forward and one is back, with the cranks horizontal. Get the weight of your body positioned over the pedals and rest

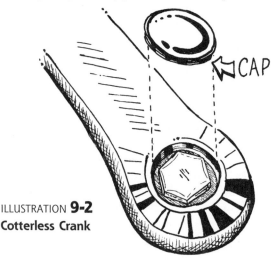

ILLUSTRATION **9-2**
Cotterless Crank

your hands on the pedals, one on each. This may require sticking one hand, arm, and shoulder through the diamond of the frame, but most mountain bike frames are small enough that you can reach over the top tube. When you're all set, push down sharply on both pedals at the same time with your hands, putting all your weight behind the push. Feel anything give? Watch the joint of each crank and the bottom bracket axle as you push down in order to determine which crank is loose. You may have to rotate the cranks 180 degrees and do the test again. It may take three or four tests, or you may not be able to tell accurately which crank is loose. But if you feel that give or hear the squeak of the crank shifting on its axle, tighten the crank bolt you suspect most, and tighten both bolts if you're not sure which one is loose.

To tighten your crank, first remove the dust cap over the crank bolt. Usually you have to unscrew (c-cl) them by putting something pointed in two little holes and twisting carefully. (Use needlenose pliers, or two tiny allen wrenches, or two little nails, or the ends of a paper clip, whatever you can get a hold of; I even used a barb on a barbed wire fence once.) Some dust caps require that you pop them out by sticking a screwdriver or knife blade in a little slot at the edge. Take care not to destroy the threads in the crank that are under the dust cap, whatever you do. Those threads are crucial for crank removal.

When you have the dust cap off, fit the socket tool over the bolt head or nut inside the crank. Make sure the tool fits well. If you are using the socket tool that's part of your Cool Tool, make sure it is snug on the crank bolt or nut, then fit the adjustable wrench on the flats of the socket and hold the socket in place with your thumb while you turn the wrench. Tighten (cl) the bolt or nut thoroughly. When it gets hard to turn the wrench, place it on the bolt or nut in such a way that you are making a "closing V" with the tool handle and the crank; the idea is to set things up so you can hold the crank still and lever the wrench handle toward it with the same hand. You can get the bolt or nut very tight by this method if you take it slow and steady. Just make sure you don't apply so much leverage to the wrench that you strip the threads on the bolt or nut.

When your crank bolt or nut is tight, you can ride in peace. You can put the dust cap back on if you want, but I prefer to leave them off. Dust won't hurt the crank bolt or nut. And while I'm giving opinions, I have to say I hate it when they use nuts to hold the cranks on. If you have nuts holding your cranks on, and one or both of them came loose, make a mental note to get some thread glue (like Loctite) when you get home, and take both nuts off, apply glue to their threads, then retighten (cl) them, so they'll stay tight (if you're lucky). If you have lots of trouble with these nuts coming loose, take the whole bottom bracket set apart and replace the axle (or spindle, as many people call it) with the kind of axle that accepts crank bolts. Then throw your nut-type axle, and the nuts, in a recycling bin. Humph. I hope they make flimsy car parts out of them, as a bad karma reward.

Crank bent, knocking chainstay. If you've had a wreck and banged a pedal so hard the crank is bent and hits against the chainstay, there isn't much you can do with your portable tool kit. There is a last-ditch method you can try for a temporary fix to get you home, though, if you can just find a farm shop with a huge (18- to 24-inch) adjustable wrench. Either walk or get a tow (see page 88) to the farm, then take the pedal off the bent crank (see page 93). Wrap some heavy cloth or burlap around the end of the crank. Then turn the crank so it is pointing straight up, and lay the bike down gently on the side that doesn't have the bent crank.

Adjust the big wrench so the jaws fit snugly over the padded end of the crank. Make sure the jaws won't dig into the threaded hole for the pedal spindle. Hold the top tube of the bike down with one hand, and use the other hand to lever the handle of the wrench upward, slowly and steadily straightening the crank. If it is a strong crank, you'll have to pull really hard on that wrench. You may even have to ask a friend or the farmer's daughter to help hold the bike down while you do the bending. But do it slowly, so you don't snap the crank off or bend it too far.

When the crank is fairly close to straight, put the pedal back on, then make a mental note to take the bike to a good shop for professional straightening, or replace the crank when you get home. A bent and rebent crank is much weaker than a new one. (Though I must confess, I rode a rebent steel Magistroni crank on my old Cinelli for years.)

Bottom Bracket

PROBLEMS: *Bottom bracket loose or tight.* Either your whole bottom bracket axle is loose, so it jiggles from side to side when you pedal, or it is hard to turn the cranks at all. You have to adjust the bearing race on the left side of the bottom bracket. First take your screwdriver and set the end in one of the notches in the lockring. Tap the screwdriver with a rock, aiming the screwdriver counter-clockwise to loosen the ring. When the ring is loose, take a small allen wrench or something similar and put it in one of the small holes that are set into the end of the adjustable race or bearing cup. Turn it the way you need to in order to tighten (cl) or loosen (c-cl) it. The best way is to tighten (cl) it all the way in until it's hard to turn the cranks, then back off (c-cl) the adjustable race about an eighth of a turn. Then tighten (cl) the lockring by using the screwdriver in a notch again.

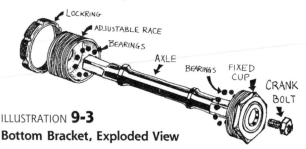

ILLUSTRATION **9-3**
Bottom Bracket, Exploded View

If the bottom bracket gets jiggly again soon, your fixed cup is probably loose. All you can do is turn it in with your fingers or maybe a narrow-jawed channel-lock pliers, if you can borrow one from a farmer or garage. The fixed cup tightens clockwise on most bikes, but counter-clockwise on some, so you have to figure out which way works on yours and get it as tight as you can manage, then ride home, keeping an eye on it. Once home, tighten it up with a tool that fits in there, or take it to a shop that will have the proper spanner for the job.

Bottom bracket noisy. If you have grindy, crackly noises coming from the front half of your power train, and you can't trace them to the pedals or cranks, chances are they are caused by grit or worn parts inside the bottom bracket. If you have some lubricant and the bearings are not sealed (you can see a little space between the bottom bracket axle and the bearing race) work a couple of drops into each side of the bottom bracket. It may help to squirt the oil onto that space between the axle and the race, then tip the bike so the lubricant runs down the axle into the works as you spin the cranks backwards. When you get some lube in there and the noises quiet down, ride home in peace, but do an overhaul when you get home, using a shop manual if you need more info. If you ride in lots of mud, sand, or salt water, consider getting a sealed-bearing bottom bracket. Those things can really last; I had a Phil Wood one that went 18 years, and it had even taken a trip to the bottom of the bay when my bike fell off a pier.

Front Sprocket or Chainwheel

PROBLEMS: *Kerchunk* sound every time the pedals go around, or the chain falls off every time it gets to a certain place on the chainwheel. Get the bike hung up on a fence post, a low limb on a tree (use a spare tube to tie it up if you need to), or your friend's willing hands. Crank the pedals slowly and watch the chain as it feeds onto the front sprocket right on the top. Does the chain kick up or jump off when it gets to one of the teeth of the sprocket each time that one tooth comes around? If so, you have a bent sprocket tooth.

If the chain doesn't kick up on any one tooth, continue cranking slowly and watch the chain where it goes through the rollers on the rear changer. Does the chain kick up or

ILLUSTRATION **9-4**
Crank and Chainwheels

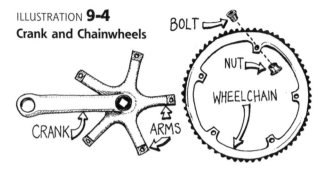

jump a little back there every once in a while? Look closely at the chain where it jumps. Is a link of the chain stuck so it doesn't flex and then straighten as it goes through the rollers? See Chain PROBLEMS if that is the case. Is the chain kicking up on one tooth of the freewheel or cassette sprockets (cogs)? If so, see Rear Sprocket PROBLEMS.

If you have a *bent tooth* on your front sprocket or chainwheel, you have to play dentist. Mark the tooth that the chain kicks up on, or jumps off of. You can just make a fingernail mark in the grease if you don't have a marker handy.

Take the chain off the chainwheel, then spin the cranks slowly and look down from directly above the chainwheel. Watch that you don't bonk your chin with a pedal, but also watch closely for the marked tooth as it comes over the top of the chainwheel. Can you see which way it's bent compared to the ones on either side? If you can't see any bend in the tooth, look at it from the side of the bike. If it's chipped or badly worn down, you have to ride home or to a good bike shop to replace the whole chainwheel.

But if you find that the tooth is simply bent a little to one side, put your adjustable wrench on the bent tooth and tighten it up so the jaws are snug against both sides. Bend the tooth a bit at a time. Take the wrench off now and then to see how you are doing. If the sprocket is a high-quality forged aluminum one, it will be hard to bend, but you can do it with patience and a firm but steady touch. If, in your efforts to straighten one tooth, you bend the whole chainwheel a bit, see *Front sprocket wobbles*, below.

When you get the tooth straight, put the chain back on and try the slow pedaling test again. If the chain runs smoothly, congrats! If not, check for another bent tooth or maybe a tight link in the chain.

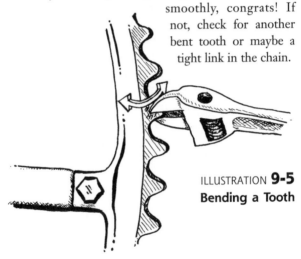

ILLUSTRATION **9-5**
Bending a Tooth

Front sprocket wobbles. This is an annoying problem. It means that one side of the chain or the other always rubs the cage of the front gear changer, no matter how well you adjust it. Prop the bike up so it won't fall over, then crank the pedals backwards slowly while you look down on the chainwheels from above. Find the area of the sprocket that bends in or out and makes the chain rub the changer cage. Mark the bent area of the sprocket with some grease from the chain if you don't have a marker with you. Sometimes it's hard to tell whether the chainwheel is bent in on one side, or out on the other. Try to decide where the majority of the chainwheel is, and call the rest bent. Does the bent area you marked fall near one of the crank arms that hold the chainwheel to the crank? Usually a bent chainwheel has been caused by a bent crank arm (spider) or a bad connection between the arm and the chainwheel (see Illustration 9-4).

Make sure all the bolts that hold the chainwheel to the crank arms are tight. Then find a chunk of wood that will butt up against the side of the crank arm where your bend is. A short section of a tree limb that has been sawed for firewood is ideal; a hunk of two by four is great, too, but I don't ride around construction projects if I can help it. Place your chunk of wood against the crank arm that is bent, then give the other end of the chunk of wood a solid whack with a fist-sized rock. You may have to lay the bike down on one side to do this properly. Check to see if you've straightened the chainwheel after your first whack. Rotate the cranks a bit if you have to take another whack, so you don't wreck the bottom bracket bearings. If a minor wobble persists, you may have to do some multi-tooth dental work with your adjustable wrench, as described in the *bent tooth* section above; just push the jaws of the adjustable wrench on further than you did to straighten a single tooth. If you get the chainwheel close to straight but not perfect, don't worry about it; as long as the chain doesn't throw or rub on the changer every time it goes around, you've done a good job.

10
Chain

PROBLEMS: *Chain thrown.* Your chain has come off the chainwheel and/or the rear sprocket. You probably need to adjust your gear changers, but use this section to get your chain back on the sprockets and to check the chain for looseness and lack of lubricant.

If the chain is jammed on either side of the freewheel or cassette sprockets, you have to grab (yuch!) the upper section of chain, just forward from those rear sprockets, then yank up as you slowly rotate the rear wheel forward. You can do this by rolling the bike forward slowly as you pull the chain free. If the chain threw off the highest (smallest) sprocket, you may have to loosen the rear wheel quick-release to free the jammed chain.

To get your chain back on the bike, put it on the rear sprocket first. Put the rear changer in its high gear position, then make sure the chain goes through both of the rollers, making a backwards "S" shape. Get it to run from the top roller onto the smallest sprocket, and all the way around that sprocket so it goes straight forward off the top. Put a friend's bike in high gear and take a look if you're not sure how it should look.

When the chain is set on the smallest rear sprocket, pull the length of chain that comes off the top of the rear sprocket tight, then press a couple of links down over the teeth at the top of the front sprocket or chainwheel. Crank the pedals forward with one hand while holding the links on the chainwheel teeth with the other hand. You have to walk along next to the bike as it rolls forward. The rest of the chain will pop onto that chainwheel.

Read the rest of the PROBLEMS in this Chain section and find out what made the chain jump off. If the chain is OK, check your gear changer adjustment, then check the front and rear sprockets for wobbles or damaged teeth.

Squeaky or gunky chain. You haven't lubricated or cleaned it in a while. It's easy to forget. But you pay heavily for that negligence on a long ride; a dry or dirty chain wastes a lot of your energy.

Before putting lubricant on the chain, see how dirty it is. If it is coated with mud or grime and the stuff is not dry, take a rag or the edge of your shirt tail, hold it loosely around the top section of chain between the front and rear sprockets, and run the pedals backwards so the chain slides through the cleaning rag. This will usually take enough of the gunk off to make the chain usable.

To lubricate the chain, get out your bike lubricant if you have some, or borrow a can of light motor oil from a farmer or garage (everybody has their own favorite lubricant, but plain old oil works OK in a pinch). Lie the bike down on its left side, then pick up the back wheel. Hold onto a seat stay with one hand, then spin the back wheel backwards, so the chain feeds backwards over the rear sprocket and through the rollers. While the chain is feeding over the back sprocket, dribble lubricant on it. If it slows to a stop, give the back wheel another backwards spin and dribble more lubricant on, until you're sure all the links of the chain have gotten a dose. Squirt a bit of lube in each roller where it spins on its axle. You don't have to work the lubricant in or anything; that'll happen as you ride. In fact if there's extra oil dripping off the chain, wipe it off with a rag; extra lubricant picks up dust and grit, which can raise the co-efficient of friction higher than the oil lowers it. Not good.

When you get back on the bike after lubricating the chain, you'll notice an incredible improvement in the ease of pedaling and gear shifting. Remember that. Keep the chain lubricated from now on. And clean the chain with a wire brush when you get home from any particularly muddy or gritty ride.

Chain sucking. This variation on a thrown chain usually happens when you are having lots of fun. That means, you are going fast, getting squirrely, drifting half out of control, giggling as you pedal for all you are worth. Then, all of a sudden, GRRAAACK! The chain gets sucked between the innermost sprocket and the chainstay or a brake arm (if you have brakes mounted under your chainstays).

It's a drag when it happens. It sucks, as they say. If the chain stays stuck in there when you stop pedaling, backpedal and it should pop free.

A number of things can cause chain suckage, but the most common causes are loose chain flapping around, or a bent sprocket, or the use of inappropriate gears. First off, don't use the smallest chainwheel when you are riding downhill. It makes the chain run loose, and puts it in very close proximity to the chain-suckage danger area, that narrow gap between the small sprocket and the chainstay. Next, check your sprockets for wobbles or bent teeth (see Sprocket PROBLEMS). If you have oval chainwheels, ride home carefully, then consider changing those oval chainwheels for round ones. Oval chainwheels increase chain flap. If you have a rear brake that's mounted under your chainstays, make a mental note to get a "shark tooth" when you get back to civilization. It's a little gizmo that keeps the chain away from the suckage zone.

Chain death. The chain falls between two of the chainwheels and gets stuck in there. This is usually due to one of two problems: you are using a narrow chain and chainwheels made for a wider chain, or your chainwheels are either bent or not bolted together properly, so there is a gap between them. You can fix a bent or loose chainwheel (see Front Sprocket PROBLEMS), but if the chainwheels and chain are mismatched sizes, you have to ride home slow and easy, then go to a shop and replace one or the other.

Loose chain. Your chain sags down between the front and rear sprockets, especially when you are using the small chainwheel. This is a bad problem, and can lead to chain suckage, chain throwing, chain death, and other masochistic chain acts I refuse to describe. So to get rid of that sag and have a longer, healthier life with your chain, take out a link or two, as described in *Tight or bent links* below. To see how many links you need to remove, put the bike in the gear that runs the chain from the biggest chainwheel to the biggest rear sprocket. Now, I know folks say that we shouldn't use this gear, but sometimes, in a pinch, we use it, so the bike should be able to accommodate. When you get the bike into this gear, see if you can make a fold in the lower section of the chain between the tension roller and the chainwheel without stretching the rear changer arm forward all the way to the limit. If you can, take out as many links as you can fold over themselves.

ILLUSTRATION **10-1**

Two Different Chain Links

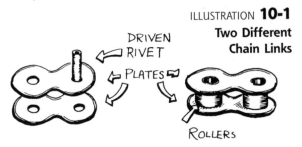

DRIVEN RIVET

PLATES

ROLLERS

Tight or bent links. When one part of your chain goes over the rear sprocket (especially a small rear sprocket) and through the rollers, the chain kinks, and then doesn't come unkinked. Or it jumps and kerchunks as it passes over the sprocket. The kink indicates a tight link; the jumping and kerchunking indicates a bent or damaged link of the chain.

If you suspect that you have a *tight link*, get the bike up off the ground and crank the pedals slowly. Watch the chain as it goes over the rear sprocket and through the rollers. See the chain jump a little each time a particular link comes around? That's your tight link. Flex the jumpy area of the chain with your fingers until you find the one that doesn't want to flex. Mark it with a little scratch on the side plate so you don't lose it.

Try to loosen the tight link up by putting a little lubricant on it and working it back and forth with your fingers. Flex it not only up and down, but side to side, so you loosen up the joints between the rivets and the rollers.

Look closely at the tight link and the ones around it. Is there a twist in the chain at your tight link? If so, get two adjustable wrenches (you *are* riding with a friend who's got one, I hope) and adjust the wrenches carefully so they squeeze the side plates of the links to either side of the twisted one. Then twist the two wrenches gently, against the bend, so it straightens out. It's amazing how often you can get the thing pretty close to straight, or at least straight enough to loosen up the tight link and ride home without throwing your chain over and over.

If you can't get your tight link loose by the above methods, get out your chain tool and set the rivet of the tight link in the slot on the chain tool that's for spreading links, as shown in Illustration 10-2. Turn the point of the tool in (cl) until it pushes against the rivet, then *carefully* turn it a little more, so it spreads the link plates a hair or two. That should be enough to loosen them from the roller, but not enough to pop the plates off the rivet. When the link is loose, lubricate it and the rest of the chain, so you don't have to deal with other tight links.

You have to *remove a link* if all your efforts fail to loosen it up, or if it is really damaged badly, or if you want to shorten the chain to get rid of looseness. Just put the link

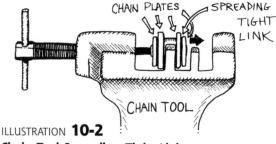

ILLUSTRATION **10-2**
Chain Tool Spreading Tight Link

you want to remove in the driving-out slot, as shown in Illustration 10-3, then screw (cl) the point of the tool in until it drives the rivet out. Make sure the point is butted up square on the end of the rivet as you drive it out. Drive the thing until the end of the rivet that is *farthest* from the point of the tool is almost flush with the outer of the edge of the casing of the chain tool, then *stop!* Don't drive the rivet all the way out of the chain or you'll never get it back in. Back (c-cl) the point of the chain tool all the way out of the hole in the chain. Take the chain out of the slot in the tool. Does the chain come apart? If not, hold the chain on either side of the driven-out rivet so it is pointing away from you. Then curve both sides of the chain towards you so that the plates spread a bit and release the driven-out rivet. Don't bend the chain hard or you'll misshape the plates. Drive out another rivet so you remove one or more complete links, and wind up with two chain ends that can fit back together. Stick these ends together and drive the rivet home; to do this you have to put the link in the driving slot of the tool, as shown in Illustration 10-3, but with the point of the tool backed (c-cl) way out to make room for that

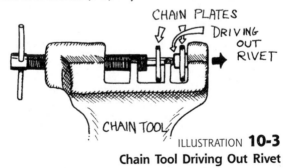

ILLUSTRATION **10-3**
Chain Tool Driving Out Rivet

protruding rivet. Drive the rivet all the way in, until the ends are flush with the outer sides of the sideplates. This takes a gentle touch. If the newly-driven rivet is tight, try to loosen it by using the methods described at the beginning of this *Tight or bent links* section.

Chain worn, or lots of kerchunking. Your chain has seen a lot of hard service, and maybe you replaced the rear sprockets but not the chain. The chain is probably so worn and stretched that it won't fit onto the sprocket teeth properly, so it jumps and kerchunks every time you pedal hard, especially in high gears. To make sure it is a worn chain causing the trouble, just pull on one of the links that are wrapped around the front of the chainwheel. If the chain pulls away from the chainwheel until you can see some of the tips of the teeth under it, your chain is worn out and ready for replacement. Lubricate the chain if it is dry, and take it easy as you ride home. Then get a replacement chain and put it on. Let's hope, by the time you read this and need a chain, that there is a good one available. I sure miss the good old Sedis Sport 3/32-inch-wide chain that used to be such a reliable standard among cyclo-crossers.

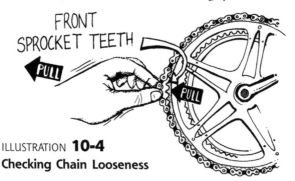

ILLUSTRATION **10-4**
Checking Chain Looseness

11
Back Half of Power Train & Gear Changers

Rear Sprockets

PROBLEMS: *Kerchunk.* Your chain kicks up about twice for every revolution of the pedals. It makes a most annoying jerk if you're pedaling hard. Check first to make sure the kerchunk isn't due to a faulty chain or chainwheel. See the PROBLEMS sections for those parts to fix them. Then check to see if weeds or twigs have wrapped around the freewheel or cassette. If you find debris clogging your sprockets, pull it out or use a screwdriver turned edgewise to scrape between the sprockets as you turn the pedals forward. If the sprockets are clear of debris but still cause the chain to kerchunk, look for worn down, chipped, or bent teeth on the sprockets. Look closely at the "U" shape between adjacent teeth. If the chain jumps on a given sprocket, especially one of the smallest sprockets, it may well be that the spaces between the teeth are worn in wider (the teeth are worn narrower, in other words) than those on other sprockets. If your rear sprockets are worn or damaged, all you can do is ride home or to a shop for cassette or freewheel replacement.

Gear Changers

DIAGNOSIS: As with brakes, gear changer systems are made up of three units: the lever, the cable, and the changer or derailleur mechanism itself. Different problems are liable to be caused by each of the different units, but many common problems require that you treat the changer system as a whole. Test the gear system for each of the following problems, then follow the procedure indicated.

PROBLEMS: If your gears are *shifting roughly*, or *not going into gear* when you shift, and you have an indexed (click-shifter) system, first try a little *Indexed system fine-tuning* as described on page 120. If that doesn't help, do the full *Changer System Adjustment* procedure in this section.

If you have *gear slippage*, particularly a tendency of the chain to slip from a large sprocket to a smaller one, either front or rear, then you are probably using a friction control lever, and the lever is probably loose. Tighten the pivot bolt of your gear lever; it's the bolt the lever pivots around, and there is usually a way to adjust how firmly it holds the lever still after you shift gears.

If your *chain is throwing*, find out if it throws off a front or a rear sprocket, then do the part of the *Changer System Adjustment* that applies to that half of the system, then see Front Changer PROBLEMS or Rear Changer PROBLEMS. Two hints can save you from many chain throwing problems: *Don't ever drop or put your bike down on its tender right side, and don't ever backpedal while shifting the gears!*

If your *chain rubs the front changer* all the time, first fiddle a bit with the lever for the front changer and see if you can move the cage enough to clear the chain. If that doesn't help, see *rubbing* on page 122. If grinding noises persist even when the front changer is adjusted, see Front Sprocket PROBLEMS.

If you do all the things above and still have a grindy or jumpy gear system, you may simply be using a combination of sprockets that your bike isn't up to using. On many bikes, it isn't easy for the chain to run from the biggest front sprocket (chainwheel) to the biggest rear sprocket, or from the smallest front sprocket to the smallest rear sprocket. The chain runs at too sharp an angle; it is either stretched very tight or sagging very loose, too. It's a strain on the whole system, and it lets you know by making unhappy noises and jumping off the sprockets. Now, in a jam, anybody can make the oversight of shifting into one of those gear combinations. We all do it now and then. But the point is that you should shift out of those extreme sprocket combinations as soon as you can; the gears achieved by those combinations can be nearly matched by other combinations of sprockets, anyway.

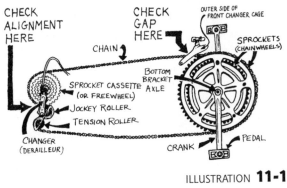

ILLUSTRATION **11-1**
Changer Adjustment

Changer system adjustment. OK. This is the procedure to follow if your gears aren't working smoothly, and you have already tried a little fine tuning (page 120). On many indexed gear systems, if you have shifting problems, you have to run through the whole procedure to catch the cause of the problem, or to correct a combination of causes. So don't try to randomly fiddle with parts of the gear system; follow this procedure in the order presented, and you'll lick your problem before you're through.

The procedure involves putting the bike in the highest gear and adjusting both front and back changers, then putting the bike in its lowest gear and adjusting the changers again. Adjusting the whole gear system is no small feat. Don't cut corners. At least check each adjustment as you go through the steps. If you aren't familiar with the names of the different parts of your changer system, look at Illustration 11-1 to get an overview. Then look at the changer and control lever illustrations later in this chapter. When you can find the cable anchor bolts are on your changers, and identify the range screws, then start the adjustment procedure. If your system is made up of a mixed set of parts, like a lever unit made by one company and a changer made by someone else, it is unlikely that you will be able to get things running smoothly. You'll probably just have to find some one gear that works and limp home, then go to a shop and get parts that are all of the same type, or certifiably interchangeable. It is a crying shame that there is so little standardization in gear systems, but that is the situation, and crying won't fix it. If we, as consumers, can find certifiably interchangeable parts, we should buy them; that is the only way we can discourage this incompatible component crap.

To start your changer system adjustment, get the bike up off the ground, or at least have a friend hold the rear wheel up. If you are adjusting an indexed system, set the control lever to *friction* mode. There's usually a little mark for friction mode, and a way to switch into it (push a little button or twist the round cap of the lever unit). You'll know you're in friction mode when you can move the control lever and not hear any clicks. Some systems, especially under-the-bar push-button ones don't allow you to switch into friction mode. This is a pain, but the procedure is still the same otherwise; you just have to put up with the clicks and some uneven gears until things are adjusted.

Turn the pedals forward and shift the bike into its highest gear. That means the gear where the chain runs on the largest front sprocket (chainwheel) and the smallest rear sprocket (cog). If the chain throws off either sprocket, feed it back on by hand and move the control lever a bit if you have to in order to make it stay there.

If you are able to get the chain to stay on the largest front and smallest rear sprocket, skip the next paragraph and get on with the adjustment.

If your changers cannot put the chain onto the highest gear sprockets, the cables might be too tight or loose. If the front changer cable is too loose, until you can pull the lever all you want and it won't push the chain onto the big sprocket, push the lever the other way, so the chain goes onto the smallest front sprocket. Then loosen (c-cl) the cable anchor bolt on the front changer and tighten up the cable until there is just a smidgen of slack left, then tighten (cl) the anchor bolt and shift that baby into high gear, so the chain is on the biggest front sprocket, where you wanted it. If the rear changer is unable to shift the chain onto the smallest sprocket, first turn the adjusting sleeve all the way in (cl) and back it out (c-cl) about two turns. If that doesn't help, loosen (c-cl) the cable anchor bolt and loosen the cable a bit, so the changer can shift the chain onto that smallest sprocket. Tighten (cl) the cable anchor bolt, leaving *no* extra slack. OK; you should now have the chain running on the biggest front sprocket and the smallest rear one. What's that? You *still* can't get into the highest gear, even with the cable tension adjusted? The changers need range adjustment. Read on; that's the next step.

To *adjust the changers in highest gear*, start with the front one and get it aligned, then adjusted. Look down on the changer cage from above. What you should see, when you're in that high gear position, is the outer side of the changer cage aligned so that its central portion is parallel with the big chainwheel, and adjusted so the outer side-plate of the cage is just missing the outer side of the chain.

First make sure the cage is lined up parallel to the chainwheel. Look down on the changer and shift it to a lower gear. With the chain off that big sprocket, you should be able to eyeball the plane of the outer side of the changer cage and the plane of the chainwheel, and see if they are parallel. If the changer is mounted askew on the seat tube, so the front end of that outer side of the cage either aims toward the bike or away from it, the changer won't work right. Sometimes the forward end of the side of the cage is purposely tweaked in a little, and sometimes there may be a jog in the cage shape near the back end of it, but that's not what concerns you. The central part of the cage, nearest to the mounting bridge that holds it to the rest of the changer, *that's* the part that has to be parallel to the chainwheel. See

Illustration 11-3. If that section isn't parallel to the chain-wheel, shift the front changer into the lowest gear (smallest sprocket) and loosen (c-cl) the mounting bolt that holds the whole changer to the bike frame. Twist the whole changer back and forth a little bit at a time, until the outer cage is lined up in a parallel plane with the big chainwheel. Make sure the changer doesn't slip up or down the frame tube; that outer cage needs to be set so it clears the big chainwheel by about ⅛ inch or so, as well as being in a parallel plane. When the cage is lined up right, and is still at the right height, tighten (cl) the changer mounting bolt firmly.

Once you have aligned the front changer, put it back in high gear, so the chain is on the biggest chainwheel, and check for a little clearance between the outer side of the chain and the outer side of the changer cage. See Illustration 11-1 for where the gap is. There should be a gap of about 1/16 of an inch, or the width of a standard pencil lead. Not much, in other words. If the gap is too big, tighten (cl) the high range screw on the front changer. If the outer side of the cage is hitting the chain, or if you couldn't even get the changer to push the chain up onto the biggest chain-wheel, loosen (cl) the high range screw. The high range screw is usually the one that's farthest from the seat tube. Use a small screwdriver to adjust it. The surest way to get the adjustment right is to loosen (c-cl) the screw enough so you can move the changer with the control lever to get that 1/16 inch gap between the cage and the chain, then tighten (cl) the high range screw until you see or feel the end of the screw touch the body of the changer. On good changers like the Sun Tour one you can look right in there and see the point of the screw. After turning it in until it touches, back off (c-cl) the screw a quarter turn or less. That should adjust the high range perfectly.

To adjust the rear changer high range, kneel or sit down behind the bike, on the right side, and look forward at the changer. It should be feeding the chain up onto the smallest rear sprocket. Find the high range screw; it is usually marked with an "H." If the screw head isn't marked, or if the H is so small and covered with dirt you can't see it, you have to peer inside the changer body and figure out which of the two range screws has its tip closest to touching the corresponding nub on the changer body. The tip of the low range screw should be far away from its nub. The tip of the high range screw may even be hidden by the nub it is touching or almost touching. At any rate, when you locate the high range screw, turn it in (cl) until the tip touches the nub on the changer body, then back it off (c-cl) about a half turn. Now look at the changer from the back of the bike and see if the chain is feeding straight up from the jockey roller of the changer onto the smallest rear sprocket. If you have something straight, like a pump, you can line it up with the smallest sprocket, as the ruler is lined up in Illustration 11-2. If the changer is out too far, or not far out enough, adjust the high range screw until things are lined up right. If the rollers are out of line, so the chain has to bend to go onto the smallest sprocket, you need to align the changer or the back end of your frame. You can try to do this by putting an allen wrench in the pivot bolt for the changer (the bolt that holds the whole thing to the drop-out) and levering either up or down on the allen wrench, but this rarely gives you enough leverage to get things aligned. If you are unable to align the rear changer, just adjust it as well as you can, ride home, then take the bike to a first-rate shop and see if they can do it with their special tools and techniques; sometimes you have to just replace the changer, if it is so bent it won't align properly.

RULER
IN LINE
WITH SMALL
SPROCKET
AND
BOTH ROLLERS

ILLUSTRATION **11-2**
**Rear Changer in High Gear
(Back View)**

When you have adjusted the changers as well as you can in their highest gear, it's time to put the whole system in its lowest gear. That means shifting the chain to the smallest front sprocket and the largest rear sprocket. If the chain throws off either sprocket, feed it back on by hand and adjust the control lever so it stays on. If the chain can't make it onto one of the sprockets, you may half to loosen (c-cl) one of the low range screws a bit, or adjust one of the cables. If the rear changer can't get the chain onto the biggest sprocket even when you pull the lever as far as it will go, you have to put the changer back in the high gear and tighten the cable. If the front changer won't let the chain go down to the smallest sprocket, you might have to loosen the cable to the front changer. In either case, loosen (c-cl) the anchor bolt, adjust the cable length, and retighten (cl) the anchor bolt.

To *adjust both changers' low range*, check the low range screws. First adjust the one on the front changer so there is a 1/16-inch gap between the inner side of the chain and the inner side plate of the changer cage. Then go back to the back of the bike and adjust the low range screw on the rear changer so the chain feeds straight up from the changer rollers onto the biggest rear sprocket. Now run through all the gears and see if they work well.

If you have an indexed system, switch the round thingie on the lever from friction into index mode and see if the clicks match the shifts of the changer. If they don't, do a little fine tuning, as follows.

Indexed system fine-tuning. If you have aligned and adjusted your indexed system as explained above, you still may have a bit of roughness in the shifting. Make sure the system is in its indexed mode, then put the front changer in the highest gear, and the rear changer in the second highest gear if its a Shimano system, or the highest gear (smallest rear sprocket) if its a Sun Tour or other system. Crank the pedals around with one hand, and turn the adjusting sleeve at the rear changer counterclockwise until you just begin to hear the chain pinging against the next lower (larger) sprocket, as if it wants to shift onto that sprocket. Then turn the adjusting sleeve back in (cl) about a quarter turn or so. Try shifting through all the gears. It may take a quarter turn more or less to zero in on the optimum cable tension for your system. If you have trouble shifting the rear changer into lower gears, you may have to adjust the angle of the dangle of the changer. Try turning the angle screw in (cl) a turn or two. This should pivot the changer down and back, so there's more room between the jockey roller and those large rear sprockets. Just don't turn that screw in too far; the changer body is supposed to be roughly horizontal, and the jockey roller should always be within a quarter inch of the rear sprocket teeth.

If shifting is still rough after fine tuning, there must be some other problem. Make sure the cables are held firmly in the anchor bolts; that's a common cause of recurrent gear problems. The cable may also be sticky and gunked up with mud or grit; clean and lubricate it. The cable housing may be kinked; straighten the kink with your hands. The cable may be old and frayed; check near the ends for this problem; if you find frayed cable, get the system in a middle gear that's usable and don't shift it again, all the way home. Then replace the cable. The changer may be clogged with dirt or rust; clean and oil the joints. Your control lever may be loose or damaged; tighten the pivot bolt on it if you can, or limp home and get a replacement for the whole lever unit. (They used to make levers you could work on, but alas, those days are gone.) The front or rear sprockets may be bent, chipped, or worn down; see Front Sprocket and Rear Sprocket PROBLEMS. The chain may be loose or shot; see Chain PROBLEMS. If the bike has been in a bad wreck and the frame is bent, or if the rear wheel or the front half of the drive train have been replaced, the chain line may be off. There's nothing you can do about this out in the wilds. Just find a gear that works and ride home in it, then take the bike to a top-notch shop that can take on a complex problem like a messed-up chain line.

Front Changer

PROBLEMS: *Rubbing.* The cage of the front changer rubs against one side or the other of the chain and makes a bothersome noise. First try to eliminate the noise with the control lever. Shifting the rear changer sometimes necessitates adjustment of the front one. Make sure the adjustable bolt on the control lever is tight enough if you have a friction system.

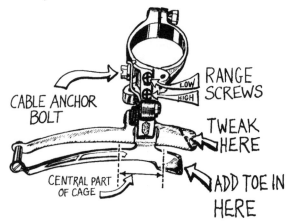

ILLUSTRATION **11-3**
Front Changer

Chain still rubbing the front changer, no matter how you set the lever? Get the bike up on a fence post, or get a friend to hold the rear wheel up, and put your head above the front changer. Crank the pedals forward slowly and watch the chain where it passes between the sides of your front changer cage. You may see a wobble in your sprocket every time it goes around. If so, go to the Front Sprocket PROBLEMS. If the chain hits because it is running at a very sharp angle from the front to rear sprockets, you are using an extreme gear position that isn't practical (see page 113).

The next thing to check out is the alignment and adjustment of the changer. See page 114 for a good procedure for doing that. If the changer is aligned correctly on the bike and adjusted properly, but the sides of the cage are bent or twisted out of the vertical plane, get out your adjustable wrench and adjust the jaws so they just slip onto the bent side plate. Bend the plate with care and patience, until it is as near to straight and vertical as you can get it; if somebody else you are riding with has a similar front changer, look at theirs to get an idea of how yours is supposed to look.

Chain throwing, or changer won't shift chain. When you shift the front changer, it either throws the chain right off the sprockets, or it won't move the chain enough to get it on the largest or smallest sprocket.

First check the alignment and adjustment of the front changer, as described on page 114. If you do that but your chain still tends to throw off the big chainwheel when you try to shift into it, do this neat trick: slip your adjustable wrench jaws onto the front tip of the outer side plate of the cage, and bend the tip in very slightly—only ¹⁄₁₆ of an inch or so. This slightly toed-in cage tip will catch a chain that has throwing tendencies.

If your adjusted and aligned front changer can't get the chain *onto* the big chainwheel, you may be able to slip your adjustable wrench jaws onto the front end of the *inner* side plate of the cage, and tweak it so the bottom edge of the inner plate bends outward (away from the bike) at the front end. Place the jaws of your adjustable wrench at the location indicated by the diagonal dotted line in Illustration 11-3. This is a subtle bend, a sort of twist, and many front changers have bends, lumps, or odd nodules at their front ends that get in your way, but if you can make a little twist at the front edge of the cage, it will flip the chain upward when you shift, so it goes onto the big chainwheel more easily. Just don't bend the whole cage out of line in your customizing efforts.

If your front changer is adjusted, aligned, and customized nicely at the front end, but the chain *still* throws off, not just when you shift, but also when you go over bumps in the middle of turns and things like that, you might have a very old, loose, or bent chain. See Chain PROBLEMS.

Rear Changer

PROBLEMS: *Chain throwing.* First make sure the rear changer is aligned and adjusted, as described on page 118. Then make sure it is attached to the frame firmly by its mounting bolt, and not bent. You can straighten some minor bends, for instance if the arm that holds the tension roller is bent a little, but major bends require that you simply limp home in any gear that works, and consult a

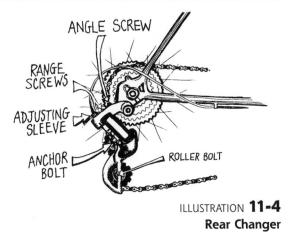

ILLUSTRATION **11-4**
Rear Changer

good shop or a shop manual for help. If the changer is so badly bent that no gears work, see *Changer Wrecked*.

Changer Wrecked. Ran over a stick and it got jammed through the chain into the spokes? Whew. That really does a number on the rear changer. Or maybe you just slammed on your right side, and the changer hit a rock. Whatever the reason, the result is the same; you have no gears now. All you can do is take out your chain tool and remove a bunch of links from the chain. The idea is to make it short enough to run from the middle front chainwheel directly to and from one of the middle rear sprockets, providing you with one gear and bypassing the broken changer. If any links of the chain got bent or broken in the mishap, make sure you remove those and leave the good links. See Chain PROBLEMS for the procedure used to take links out of the chain. If you can't get the wrecked changer off the bike, at least tie it up to the seat or chain stay to keep it from flapping around and wreaking more havoc in the spokes. When you get home on your one-speed (amazing, isn't it, how well you can get along with just one speed, if you don't hurry?) you'll have to get a new changer, and maybe a new chain, if parts of the old chain got twisted in the action.

Postscript

Hey, I had fun writing this book. I've been riding around in the boonies for over forty years, and I have always loved the great feeling of independence from civilization and the interdependence with all the plant people, animal people and insect people in the back country. And you know, when something breaks down, sometimes that gives you your best chance to sit still and tune in to all the relatives we have out there.

In fact, I think I'll go for a ride, right now. If something breaks or gets messed up on my bike, I'll let you know about it in my next revision.

If you have some problem on a ride, and find out I didn't cover it well enough in this little book, I'd sure appreciate it if you'd write the publisher and let me know. If there's one thing that can give you almost as much pleasure as being independent and free out there in the boonies, it's sharing some neat trick you've learned to maintain your independence, thereby helping somebody else in that direction. Know what I mean?

INDEX

TERRAGRAPHICS bicycling books you may enjoy:

TOURING THE WASHINGTON DC AREA
BY BICYCLE

National monuments, off-road urban trails, and rural routes in
the Blue Ridge Mountains. $10.95 paper, 174 pages

TOURING NEW ENGLAND BY BICYCLE

One- to five-day loops through this picturesque region. $10.95
paper, 174 pages

TOURING THE SAN FRANCISCO BAY AREA
BY BICYCLE

Hundreds of miles of cycling roads, from northern Marin County
to Santa Cruz. $10.95 paper, 174 pages

TOURING CALIFORNIA'S WINE COUNTRY
BY BICYCLE

Includes wine-tasting opportunities throughout Northern California. $10.95 paper, 174 pages

TOURING SEATTLE BY BICYCLE

A variety of rides in the Puget Sound area. $10.95 paper, 174
pages

TOURING THE ISLANDS

Twelve islands in the northwest Olympic Peninsula area offer a
wide variety of terrain. $10.95 paper, 174 pages

Available from your local bookstore, or order direct from the
publisher. Please include $1.25 shipping & handling for the first
book, and 50¢ for each additional book. California residents
include local sales tax. Write for our free complete catalog of over
400 books and tapes.

TEN SPEED PRESS
P. O. Box 7123   Berkeley, California 94707
(510) 845-8414